Praise for *#FormativeTech*

#FormativeTech is an incredible guide and resource for teachers who are integrating technology into their classrooms. Teachers will find useful information about assessing students successfully with technology and using this data for student success. They will also discover resources for ensuring students are learning at their best with the technology.

Shelly Sanchez Terrell, International Speaker and Author of *The 30 Goals Challenge for Teachers*

This book is a great resource for all teachers. Assessment can often be seen as a four-letter-word, but Monica Burns reminds us that if done well, it can be a tool for better supporting student learning and creating student empowerment. *#FormativeTech* is approachable and full of "use it on Monday" ideas. I can't wait to share this with my colleagues!

Jennie Magiera, Educator and Author of *Courageous Edventures*
Chief Technology Officer for Des Plaines
School District 62
Chicago, IL

Monica Burns is savvy about teaching, assessment, and how technology enhances both. Her deep expertise on the subject and knowledge of formative assessment research—through a personable, no-nonsense voice—makes her the perfect guide through these absorbing tools, tips, and anecdotes. The ideas from this super-inspiring author are ones you'll return to often.

Todd Finley, Editorial Assistant and Blogger
Edutopia
Greenville, NC

There is no better time than now to bring together the powerful learning forces of technology integration and formative assessment. This is showcased beautifully through the writing of Monica Burns in a way that is meaningful, sustainable, and scalable for teachers and leaders. This book is an ideal read for educators looking to grow more agile in their use of data to individualize and personalize instruction.

Robert Dillon, Director of Innovative Learning
School District of University City
University City, MO

As someone who's been involved in many mobile device initiatives in schools, I've seen first-hand the power devices have in informing instruction when coupled with meaningful formative assessment. In #*FormativeTech*, Monica Burns does an amazing job, not only of delving into the technology part of formative assessment, but also into the research behind what can make it most effective for learning. This book is full of tools, strategies, and lesson ideas that you can use in your classroom right away to help inform learning and make it meaningful, sustainable, and scalable.

**Carl Hooker, Director of Innovation
and Digital Learning**
Eanes Independent School District
Austin, TX

Since NCLB came into play, data has been driving instruction whether or not the teachers were able to best determine how to calculate and apply the data in real time. Often this is due to the fact that the data teachers receive is not real-time data, but rather data from the prior year that is technically out-of-date for the specific student. The other reason is simply because undergraduate classes simply do not teach how to figure the types and calculations of data that would be applicable in different situations, along with what to do with the data to improve student performance. Teachers are—and historically have been—excellent at gathering, recording, and reporting data; however that has often been the extent of their involvement with it. This book will be the ticket to board the train that gets teachers to understand progress monitoring and calculating growth, as well as what to do with the information once they have it.

Pamela L. Opel, Special Education
Instructional Specialist, 6–12
Gulfport School District
Gulfport, MS

Teachers often recognize the need for formative assessment but don't have enough "tricks in their bags" to properly employ on a routine basis. Combining formative assessment with technology can help teachers expand their repertoire while also simplifying data collection and analysis.

Christine Landwehrle, K–12
Director of Curriculum
School Administrative Unit 39
Amherst, NH

#FormativeTech

To my sister,
for whose strength and guidance I am forever grateful.

#FormativeTech

Meaningful, Sustainable, and Scalable Formative Assessment With Technology

Monica Burns

Foreword by Reshan Richards

CORWIN
A SAGE Publishing Company

FOR INFORMATION:

Corwin

A SAGE Company

2455 Teller Road

Thousand Oaks, California 91320

(800) 233-9936

www.corwin.com

SAGE Publications Ltd.

1 Oliver's Yard

55 City Road

London EC1Y 1SP

United Kingdom

SAGE Publications India Pvt. Ltd.

B 1/I 1 Mohan Cooperative Industrial Area

Mathura Road, New Delhi 110 044

India

SAGE Publications Asia-Pacific Pte. Ltd.

3 Church Street

#10-04 Samsung Hub

Singapore 049483

Printed in the United States of America

Library of Congress Cataloging-in-Publication Data

Names: Burns, Monica, 1986- author.

Title: #FormativeTech : meaningful, sustainable, and scalable formative assessment with technology / Monica Burns; foreword by Reshan Richards.

Other titles: Pound sign FormativeTech | FormativeTech

Description: Thousand Oaks, California : Corwin, 2017. | Includes bibliographical references and index.

Identifiers: LCCN 2016047020 | ISBN 9781506361901 (pbk. : alk. paper)

Subjects: LCSH: Educational evaluation—Technological innovations. | Educational tests and measurements—Technological innovations. | Students—Rating of—Technological innovations.

Classification: LCC LB2822.75 .B89 2017 | DDC 371.260285—dc23

LC record available at https://lccn.loc.gov/2016047020

This book is printed on acid-free paper.

Acquisitions Editor: Ariel Bartlett

Senior Associate Editor: Desirée A. Bartlett

Editorial Assistant: Kaitlyn Irwin

Production Editor: Amy Schroller

Copy Editor: Lana Todorovic-Arndt

Typesetter: C&M Digitals (P) Ltd.

Proofreader: Dennis W. Webb

Indexer: Sheila Bodell

Cover Designer: Anupama Krishnan

Marketing Manager: Jill Margulies

Certified Sourcing
www.sfiprogram.org
SFI-00453

17 18 19 20 21 10 9 8 7 6 5 4 3 2 1

DISCLAIMER: This book may direct you to access third-party content via Web links, QR codes, or other scannable technologies, which are provided for your reference by the author(s). Corwin makes no guarantee that such third-party content will be available for your use and encourages you to review the terms and conditions of such third-party content. Corwin takes no responsibility and assumes no liability for your use of any third-party content, nor does Corwin approve, sponsor, endorse, verify, or certify such third-party content.

Contents

Foreword

Approximately 7 years into my educational career as a middle school math teacher, I reached a point of being able to articulate my frustrations with the ways that schools measured mathematical understanding possessed by students and how many educators, and the global public, perceived assessment of learning in general.

For example, in my eighth-grade math class, we followed a very traditional Algebra 1 curriculum. (In fact, we used the same textbook that I had used when I had taken Algebra 15 years earlier!) How did I arrive at this practice? I followed the leads of other, more experienced teachers in the department who also taught eighth grade. Each meeting block had a typical rhythm: our class would go over the previous night's homework, and then I would deliver some new instruction. Students engaged in some assigned classwork, and then I would inform them of their new homework, usually due the next day. Halfway through a chapter, students would take a short quiz, and at the end of the chapter, a test. Sometimes I asked students to come up to the whiteboard and solve a problem in front of the class. Sometimes, multiple students solved a problem. Questioning, dialogue, and showing work were all encouraged of course, but when trying to "stay on track" and keep to a schedule—after all, students needed to be ready to take the generic final exam at the end of the year *and* be ready with the foundational knowledge for the next math course in their sequence—measuring what a student was able to recall always seemed to take priority over what was more important, that is, what the student was able to do with that knowledge.

I have always struggled with giving grades on quizzes and tests. Sure, grades are the most visible and easily recognized form of feedback, but they are not necessarily the most representative of what a student knows or is able to do with what he or she knows. For me, the most valuable form of feedback is individual guidance, and I tried to offer this to my students. But, due to my class sizes and the number of classes I taught, offering such valuable feedback to students felt impossible, or at least unsustainable. I felt stuck, unable to meaningfully guide my students to where I wanted them to be.

I had already been using technology for instructional delivery and for occasional predictability-shifting novelty, but it was around this frustration tipping point that I made a new intentional effort toward using technology to (1) better understand what students knew, (2) better understand what students were able to do with what they knew, and (3) better lead and guide students toward curricular and learning objectives organized around (1) and (2).

In the first year of this new intentionality, I abandoned about 50% of my traditional assessments and replaced them with screencasting activities. I already was using screencasting to record mini-lessons and review materials. I relied on an interactive whiteboard connected to a single desktop computer in my classroom, a USB external microphone, and software that could capture everything happening on the screen. One day I created the opportunity for my students to record a screencast during class, and a giant light bulb went off in my head: this was going to be how I would better capture their understanding and document and communicate how they were applying their thinking.

This moment led to my eventual research area (formative assessment with technology) and involvement in the creation of a software company to support mobile screencasting (Explain Everything). I began a long journey toward addressing my frustrations around assessment practices, while challenging norms and generating an authentic alternative worth considering.

I've known Monica Burns for many years—as a fellow New Yorker, Apple Distinguished Educator, and general EdTech enthusiast. What I find most remarkable about this book currently sitting in your hands is that it provides clear, approachable, and actionable steps for shifting practices within the greater context of systemic change in assessment practices and perceptions in today's schools. I was fortunate to be at the right place and time in my professional and academic career to connect the dots between formative assessment, technology, and learning. Because of this book, such fortune is not requisite. Any teacher who reads this book will stand a chance of making similar connections and best serving his or her students.

Sure, the technologies will change over time, but the embedded beliefs and practices brought to life through the examples and ideas in this book will always be relevant, will always be important. We can complain about high stakes testing and the superficial value of traditional grading practices, but without proposing effective and, as Monica defines, meaningful, sustainable, and scalable alternatives, the same practices will linger, and educational systems will continue to do students a disservice, confusing learning with testing and assessment with grading.

—Reshan Richards

Co-author of *Blending Leadership:*
Six Simple Beliefs for Leading Online and Off
Adjunct Faculty, Teachers College,
Columbia University and Columbia
School for Professional Studies
Co-founder and Chief Learning Officer, Explain Everything

Acknowledgments

I would like to take a moment to thank the educators from around the world who shared their stories in *#FormativeTech*. The teacher leaders you'll find sprinkled in the pages of this book took the time to talk to me about their special experiences to illustrate the use of technology for formative assessment. This includes dear friend and former colleague Tammy Musiowsky who works tirelessly to support the needs of her students.

A special thank you to the Apple Distinguished Educator community, especially Reshan Richards. Thank you Reshan for your support throughout this process. Your research and passion for this topic is truly inspiring.

And a final thank you to Corwin and my amazing editor Ariel Bartlett for embracing the potential of educational technology and supporting the *#FormativeTech* journey.

PUBLISHER'S ACKNOWLEDGMENTS

Corwin gratefully acknowledges the contributions of the following reviewers:

Mandy Frantti
Teacher, Physics/Astronomy/Mathematics
Munising Middle/High School
Munising, MI

Pamela L. Opel
Special Education Instructional Specialist, 6–12
Gulfport School District
Gulfport, MS

About the Author

Dr. Monica Burns is an EdTech and Curriculum Consultant, Apple Distinguished Educator, and Founder of Class TechTips.com. In her role as a classroom teacher in general education and integrated co-teaching settings, she used iPads one-to-one with her students, while aligning her instruction to the Common Core State Standards. Monica has presented to teachers, administrators, and tech enthusiasts at numerous national and international conferences. She is a webinar host for SimpleK12, a regular contributor to Edutopia, and author of *Deeper Learning With QR Codes* and *Augmented Reality: A Scannable Solution for Your Classroom* (Corwin, 2016).

Monica visits schools across the country to work with PreK–20 teachers to make technology integration exciting and accessible. She also provides support to organizations using technology to reach children and families in need. Monica is a graduate of the University of Delaware and Hunter College and received a doctorate in educational leadership from Lamar University.

Introduction

Meaningful, Sustainable, and Scalable Best Practices

My first year of teaching, just shy of a decade ago, was in a classroom with chalk and an overhead projector. The look and feel of my classroom changed dramatically in a relatively short period of time—from little technology in the room to an iPad in the hand of every student. I now had spreadsheets holding student data recorded just seconds before and the ability to watch screencasts where students explained the steps to solving a math problem. All within the same four walls of Room 235.

Although many of the choices I made as a teacher changed with the introduction of technology—integrating iBooks Author created textbooks, using scannable technology to differentiate instruction—my goals remained the same. I worked hard to support students as they mastered and honed new skills over the school year. Part of this work involved growing an understanding of the individual and collective needs of my students.

Purposeful formative assessment is a nonnegotiable in every classroom. The cycle of teaching new information, figuring out who understands this content, and making a plan on how to reach the child who does not, are all part of the job description. Instructing a class of 30 students in all subject areas or managing over 100 students rotating in and out over the course of the day, can make this a daunting challenge—not to mention a logistical juggling act. Collecting, analyzing, and acting on formative assessment data is a must for educators. Technology tools can make this process *meaningful*, *sustainable*, and *scalable*.

> Technology tools can make this process *meaningful, sustainable, and scalable.*

In this book, you'll find tips to implement tomorrow—quick fixes perfect for kindergarten classrooms and high school seminars. You'll picture how meaningful formative assessment connected to learning goals and embedded throughout individual lessons and units can help you understand student progress and intervene when needed. This book covers whole-class data collection and small-group support structures to help you integrate technology tools in a sustainable manner.

Technology tools can make **formative assessment**

- *meaningful* by providing opportunities to seamlessly embed data collection in everyday lessons,
- *sustainable* through routines that are customizable and efficient, and
- *scalable* by connecting information with all stakeholders as you work toward systemic change.

Chapter 1 of this book provides an overview of formative assessment. This section is designed to review the big ideas around formative assessment before diving into technology integration.

In Chapter 2, you'll learn how to get started embedding formative assessment into your instruction. This section breaks down lessons and units into *before, during,* and *after* components to help you examine your current practice and take it to the next level.

Chapter 3 provides tips and tricks for managing #FormativeTech with your whole class. It focuses on how teachers can increase efficiency in data collection through student polling, checklists, and #FormativeTech workflow systems.

Chapter 4 explains how #FormativeTech can be used when students are working independently. It provides strategies and examples of how to check student understanding and provide feedback.

In Chapter 5, you'll see how #FormativeTech can be used during long-term assignments, including project-based learning. This chapter discusses how to use benchmarks, monitor collaboration and provide opportunities for students to reflect on their learning.

Chapter 6 provides strategies for organizing and analyzing all of the data collected through #FormativeTech tools. This chapter includes tips for identifying and evaluating data for the purpose of targeted intervention.

In Chapter 7, you'll hear how #FormativeTech can make it easier to share student progress with families. These tools can help open the walls of your classroom and empower families to support their children's academic growth.

In addition to actionable ideas that are doable in classrooms with a range of technology tools, this book provides strategies for scaling formative assessment initiatives across grade levels throughout your school building. Each chapter concludes with helpful tips connected to the big idea of making #FormativeTech *meaningful, sustainable,* and *scalable.* I hope you'll find these mini-action items as quick inspiration for integrating technology into your formative assessment process.

Formative assessment rooted in best practices and elevated with the appropriate tools can have a lasting impact on teaching and learning in your classroom. As you move through this book, scan the QR codes to explore spotlight tools and follow the hashtag #FormativeTech on social media to see how teachers are energizing their practice with digital devices!

I'm so excited you're joining me on this #FormativeTech journey! Formative assessment is more than a hot topic. It's a research-based, effective teaching practice. With the thoughtful integration of technology tools, we can make formative assessment *meaningful, sustainable,* and *scalable* together!

Scan this QR code to visit the companion website with extra resources and information on #FormativeTech:

http://resources.corwin.com/formativetech

CHAPTER 1

Formative Assessment 101

The basic goal of formative assessment is straightforward: figure out what students understand and where misconceptions or gaps in understanding exist, so you can plan instruction and interventions to help students master learning objectives. In his book *Transformative Assessment,* W. James Popham (2008) provides the following definition for formative assessment: "Testing students in the midst of an ongoing instructional sequence and then using the test results to improve instruction" (p. 3). The implementation of data collection and use of data to guide instruction is definitely easier said than done. It requires planning, an understanding of student needs, and pedagogical knowledge of the best interventions for students who struggle, as well as extensions for students who excel.

Formative assessment takes many shapes, and most teachers have set routines for collecting and analyzing data to inform their instruction. This might include observations and anecdotal notes, checklists to monitor skill development, quick quizzes at the beginning of class, or exit slips before the bell rings. The purpose should always be clear no matter *when* or *how* formative assessment data is collected. Teachers know what they are looking for when they pose a question to students—and they have a plan for what to do if students don't understand.

Why do teachers collect data? They might want information on how well students understand a concept, so they can divide the class into groups for an activity. They might want a read of the room at the beginning of a class to gauge student interest before opening discussion questions. A teacher might also want to see if he or she can skip over a lesson because the class already understands a topic—or if they need to slow down to clarify misconceptions.

> The purpose should always be clear no matter *when* or *how* formative assessment data is collected.

CYCLE OF FORMATIVE ASSESSMENT

The cycle of formative assessment is ongoing. Teachers continuously check in on students to make sure they are moving toward mastery of the concepts being taught. Teachers start by introducing a concept to students and gathering information on whether or not students understand. This happens by asking questions to the whole class or individual students, listening in as students complete a task, or reviewing work at the end of an

Adapted From Laura Greenstein's *What Teachers Really Want to Know About Formative Assessment*

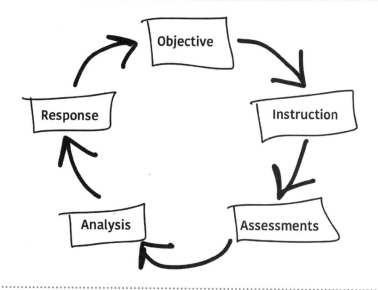

activity or lesson. Laura Greenstein (2010) describes formative assessment as a cycle: "With formative assessment, teaching and assessing become a cyclical process for continuous improvement, with each process informing the other" (p. 7).

FORMATIVE ASSESSMENT IN A TRADITIONAL CLASSROOM

Throughout this book, we'll examine the ways technology can enhance traditional formative assessment practices. In order to do this, let's *establish* a foundation for *when* and *how* formative assessment takes place in a traditional classroom where technology isn't thrown into the mix. In this section, you'll see how formative assessment data is collected before, during, and after a daily lesson, multiday activity, or unit of study. In the next chapter, we'll come back to these key points as we discuss *meaningful*, *sustainable*, and *scalable* technology integration.

Before a Lesson or Unit

In the early stages of planning a lesson teachers identify a clear objective or goal for student mastery. Planning a lesson is more than knowing what content your students need to know to pass a test. In addition to keeping your learning goals for students in mind, it is important to gauge what students already know about a concept and what misconceptions might get in the way of their understanding of new information. Before a lesson or unit, you also have an opportunity to learn about your students' interests and how they might connect to the topic you are teaching. All of this information—student understanding, misconceptions, and interests—will be useful to you use as you plan a daily lesson or month-long unit.

Questions to ask yourself:

- What do I want students to master by the end of the unit?
- How will I know if they understand a concept?
- What should I observe as I move about the classroom?
- What type of information can I collect from students to see if they have mastered a learning goal?

- How can I intervene if a student is struggling?
- What will I do if students are ready to think deeper or explore something new?
- How will I record and keep track of this formative assessment data?

For example, if you poll the class to see which nonfiction topics they like the best, you can use this data to choose informational text examples on high-interest topics like sharks or global warming when you model reading skills. In a math classroom, you might give a quick five-question quiz to students before starting the lesson. If everyone shows they understand the skill, you might use more challenging examples in your lesson or skip ahead to something new. If a few students struggle, you might work with them in a small group, while the other students work in partners to complete the daily task.

During a Lesson or Unit

As teachers move through a lesson, they should check for understanding every few minutes. This will help you decide on the direction a lesson will take, including slowing down or speeding up as you share content with students. This doesn't mean you are interrupting a lesson to give multiple-choice questions every 10 minutes. It means you are consistently monitoring students through observations, questioning, and quick review of their work.

> What does the research say? Teachers should check for understanding every 5–10 minutes to ensure rigorous, supported instruction. (Fisher & Frey, 2011)

During a lesson, you are always gathering information (aka formative assessment data). This should be done in a purposeful, planned manner. You might have questions or prompts written out in your lesson plans or identified an indicator that will tell you if students understand a specific concept. In addition to your plan for formative assessment, you know your students and when a *pulse check* is necessary. Your decision to pause and check for understanding during these *on-the-fly* moments should be in addition to plans you've made before the lesson to collect formative data at a certain time. This information will tell you who needs extra help right away and who can benefit from strategic interventions during other parts of the day or in subsequent lessons.

For example, a teacher moving around the classroom might make a note on a checklist if students are struggling to work through the steps of a science experiment with their group. Depending on what the teacher hears when she leans in to listen to a student discussion, she may decide to pause and remind the whole class of key vocabulary terms they'll need to complete the task. Alternatively, during a writing conference you might notice a student struggling to support his or her topic sentence with details. If two or three other students are struggling with this same skill, you might decide to pull them together for a strategy lesson the following day.

After a Lesson or Unit

The information collected once a lesson is finished can help teachers plan for future instruction. When reflecting on a day's lesson, you might find (1) everyone, (2) some students, or (3) none of your students *got it*. With this information, you'll decide if you are going to

- reteach a lesson with new strategies,
- slow down your lesson to dig deeper,
- differentiate by forming leveled groups of students, or
- decide on specific interventions for individual students.

The information gathered at the end of a daily lesson can help you determine what your whole-group and small-group instruction will look like in subsequent days. For example, after completing a lesson on causes of the American Revolution, tell students, "Jot down on an index card which event leading up to the American Revolution had the most impact on the colonists' decision to declare

Leveled or strategy group: a small group of students with similar needs who spend extra time with their teacher to practice a skill

independence." Collecting this at the end of the lesson will help you figure out if there are any misconceptions to address at the beginning of the next day's lesson.

At the end of a unit, you will gather information to help you plan for the next unit by noticing patterns where students may need extra support. For example, in an English Language Arts classroom, once a unit on persuasive writing is finished, you might notice a few students struggle with sentence structure or grouping ideas in paragraphs. Even though your next unit is on memoirs, this information can help you plan for small-group lessons on these basic writing skills during the following unit.

Formative assessment is more than gauging what students *don't know*. The collection of formative assessment data provides a window into student understanding. You might pose questions to students to see what they find interesting about a topic to create more engaging lessons. You can ask questions to determine if you can move through information quicker if your class already demonstrates understanding, or if you'll need to slow down to address misconceptions. With formative assessment, teachers are leading a *fact-finding mission,* and it is essential to establish *why* you are collecting data, *how* you will collect data, and *what* you will do with this information.

Table 1.1 Collecting Formative Assessment Data

Before a lesson or unit	During a lesson or unit	After a lesson or unit
• Poll the class to gauge interest	• Confer with individual students	• Collect an exit slip with student responses to a comprehension question
• Give a quick quiz on the new skill or topic to see what students already know	• Listen to group or partner talk	• Ask students to tell you something they found confusing in a lesson
• Use a KWL chart or identify misconceptions	• Ask students to write a question they have on a sticky note	• Review final projects to look for skill gaps that can be addressed in an upcoming unit

FORMATIVE vs. SUMMATIVE ASSESSMENT

When people outside of the world of education hear the term *assessment*, they picture students bubbling in answers in a silent room with desks neatly lined up. State and national exams administered at the end of the school year are called *summative assessments*. Summative assessments are the end-of-unit and end-of-year exams designed to gauge a student's understanding of course content. This information might be used to place a student in the appropriate-leveled course for the following year. It does not inform the instruction of the teacher or intervention specialists currently working with a child.

Summative tests can give teachers and districts a general feel for the effectiveness of teaching practices and curriculum material. It does not give the actionable data teachers can use to inform their instruction to meet the immediate needs of students. In this book, we will focus on *formative assessments*— how teachers can purposefully embed these types of assessments into their instruction and gather data to make decisions for teaching and learning.

Table 1.2   Examples of Formative and Summative Assessments

Formative assessment	Summative assessment
• Exit slips	• End of unit exams
• Mid-unit quizzes	• Final projects
• Conferences	• Portfolios

REIMAGINE THE CYCLE OF #FORMATIVETECH WITH TECHNOLOGY

Part of what we will discuss in this book are quick fixes for substituting traditional formative assessment practices. These quick fixes will help teachers collect data more efficiently to save instructional time. In addition to quick fixes, other aspects of the text will address large-scale changes to totally transform your practice. This includes ways to redefine how students reflect on their progress and respond to teacher feedback. It will explore reasons to embed questions into your instruction and identify opportunities for students to interact with their peers as they move through the school year. Teachers looking to build their confidence with technology tools who are just starting to wrap their head around thoughtful technology integration may want to start off with some of these simple tips as they move toward more transformative practice with #FormativeTech.

The practical changes outlined throughout the book—and the powerful teacher stories of formative assessment in action—are perfect for educators and school leaders looking to make big changes. Altering your workflow to make formative assessment happen seamlessly is all part of the process. We will build on the foundation of best practices for formative assessment introduced in this chapter by discussing how to thoughtfully integrate technology tools to make this work more meaningful, sustainable, and scalable.

TIPS FOR TODAY

- *Meaningful*: Take stock of your formative assessment practices. What are you currently doing to check for student understanding as you teach a lesson?
- *Sustainable*: Reflect on your current formative assessment practices. What is working or not working when you collect data on student understanding?
- *Scalable*: Commit to a simple goal you can put into practice tomorrow—with or without technology—such as polling for student interest or meeting with a strategy group. What is one thing you can add to your formative assessment routine?

Scan this QR code to visit the companion website with extra resources and information on #FormativeTech:

 http://resources.corwin.com/formativetech

CHAPTER 2

Transform Practice

Embedded Everyday

In the first chapter, we examined formative assessment in a traditional classroom. The purpose of this book is to demonstrate how technology can be used in a meaningful, sustainable, and scalable way to enhance formative assessment. The seminal work of Black and Wiliam (1998), as well as the continued research and writing of Corwin author Larry Ainsworth, demonstrates the impact of formative assessment on student achievement. Ainsworth (2015) describes how formative is not about gathering information for letter grades, but instead, "these assessments *for* learning yield diagnostic student feedback that educators use solely to inform and adjust instruction" (p. 33).

We've established that the collection of formative assessment data happens before, during, and after a lesson. Formative assessment should happen consistently. Teachers can continue this *fact-finding mission* throughout a lesson and unit of study: during whole-group, small-group, and one-on-one instruction. Technology tools combined with best practices for data collection and analysis make it easier to embed formative assessment into traditional lessons.

GETTING STARTED WITH #FORMATIVETECH INTEGRATION

Throughout this book, you'll find examples of how teachers are using technology tools in their classrooms: stories from my own practice and stories teachers have shared. Many examples call out specific names of products, but we all know technology evolves over time. This book is not a list of the best formative assessment tools, even though you'll find plenty of favorites to help you get started. Instead, this book provides context for examining formative assessment tools by highlighting the ways data collection and analysis has evolved as a result of education technology innovations. You might decide to search for one of the tools mentioned in this book or click on the link on the companion website. More importantly, I hope you will shift your thinking beyond a brand name to embrace a best practice.

> Shift your thinking beyond a brand name to embrace a best practice.

Let's think back to Table 1.2 in Chapter 1. In the first chapter, I described how formative assessment looks in a traditional classroom. It's time to think beyond the traditional and discover how technology tools can be used to enhance the learning experience for students—and help teachers work smarter not harder.

BEFORE A LESSON OR UNIT

As we build on the foundation of formative assessment outlined in Chapter 1, let's revisit the KWL example given in Table 1.1 where teachers ask students to identify what they know, want to know, and what they learned about a topic. There are multiple dimensions of formative assessment addressed in this example. Not only does the teacher make sure everyone is participating; but, he or she is able to get a sense of who has a depth of background knowledge and who is full of misconceptions about a topic. Teachers using formative assessment before a lesson are on a *fact-finding mission*.

> A **KWL** is an activity used before a lesson or unit to figure out what students know about a topic (K) and want to know about a topic (W). A KWL is revisited at the end of a lesson or unit to see what students learned about a topic (L).

When teachers use technology tools during a KWL, they are finding out information on student understanding that can help them (1) tailor their upcoming lessons to individual and whole-group needs, (2) form groups for learning activities, (3) address misconceptions with individual students or the entire class. This does not mean students are silently tapping answer choices on their tablet screen and waiting for the next instruction from their teacher. Teachers can ask students to think-pair-share to get their wheels spinning before entering a response into a digital tool.

Teachers can still use a KWL to prompt a discussion by posing thought-provoking questions to hook students at the beginning

A teacher asks students what they already know and gives them time to talk with peers. Students then use a digital tool to submit responses, which the teacher can review in real time.

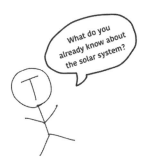

TEACHER PROMPT   **THINK-PAIR-SHARE**

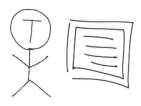

Submits response to
question with a
#FormativeTech tool

Scrolls through student responses and
adjusts instruction to address
misconceptions and leverage what
students already know

of a lesson. If your purpose for a KWL activity is to find out what students already know and want to know, technology tools can help you collect genuine responses from students to inform decisions about what will be addressed during a unit of study. Instead of a few students raising their hand, all students can submit a response for the teacher to review that will ultimately influence their instructional decisions.

The three examples listed in Table 2.1 demonstrate how teachers can use technology tools to gather information. This data is now *actionable* because you have it in real time. You can use this information in the moment to make decisions about how you will use instructional time with students.

Padlet KWL—Padlet.com is a popular option for KWL activities. After a teacher creates a board they can share the link with their students. Students then open their web browser and are able to post a short message on the Padlet board. This is a space students can use to submit responses and see the responses of their peers. Teachers can use this online space to identify what students already know about a topic and address any misconceptions they might have.

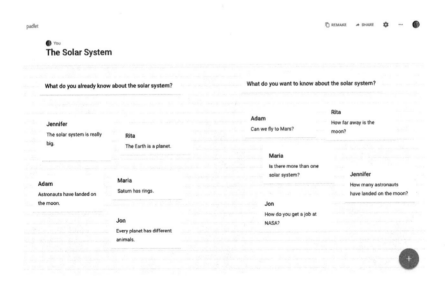

SOURCE: https://padlet.com/

A quick interest survey can help you decide how to frame an example or tell a story at the start of a lesson. If you poll the room and find out all of your students have seen the movie *The Martian*, you might incorporate it into your introduction to a lesson on sustainable farming or the solar system. If you give a survey before teaching a unit on weather systems and find out your students are most excited to learn about tornadoes, you might shift the focus of your lesson to highlight examples related to tornadoes.

With technology tools, we get a quick read of the room before the lesson. Teachers can discover student interests and use these to their advantage when introducing a unit of study. You're able to identify student misconceptions and use this information to help frame a discussion on a new topic—whether you clarify those misconceptions directly or not.

If you were collecting student poll information on an index card or sticky notes before, now you can use technology tools to make sure you've received formative assessment data from every student, right at the beginning of a lesson. Instead of *I wish I knew how much my students loved this subtopic* or *If I had known no one had read this book last year, I would have used a different example* ... you can now gather information efficiently and act on it in the moment.

Tools for KWLs:

- Padlet: Teachers create a Padlet page and students access a link provided by their teacher. Then they open this webpage on their Internet browser and can click on the screen to add a comment. Everyone with a link to the board can see student contributions.
- Google Forms: Teachers create a Google Form and share the link to the form with students. Students can then submit their responses to each question. Teacher see all of the students' responses on their screen.

Tools for Polling Students:

- Kahoot: Teachers log in to Kahoot and launch a poll. They share the virtual pin number for that session with their students. Students open Kahoot on a web browser on any device and enter the pin number to join the poll. Teachers can display results to the whole class or review responses from individual students after class.
- Nearpod: Teachers can add a poll to an interactive presentation they've made with Nearpod. When students join the Nearpod session, they can respond to poll questions teachers have embedded in their lesson. Teachers will see poll results in real time and have the option to share with their class.

Nearpod can be used to embed polls into an interactive lesson. If you know your students are excited about a particular part of the world, you can gear your instruction toward their interests.

 Which part of the world would you like to visit the most?

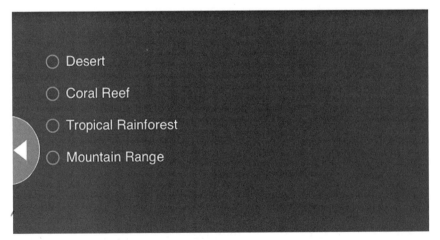

- Desert
- Coral Reef
- Tropical Rainforest
- Mountain Range

SOURCE: https://nearpod.com/

Table 2.1 Before a Lesson or Unit

In a traditional classroom	In a tech-friendly classroom	Working smarter, not harder, with technology
• Poll the class to gauge interest	• Students use their mobile device to submit answers to a set of poll questions as a *do now* at the beginning of class.	Instead of counting how many hands are raised or reviewing answers on a sheet of paper, teachers can view responses on their computer or mobile device in real time.
• Give a quick quiz on the topic/skill in the day's lesson to see what students already know	• Students answer a few multiple-choice or short response questions when they walk to the room.	The teacher knows right away who has mastered or doesn't understand the topics previously covered. Now, they can quickly decide how to group students for the day's lesson based on the quick data submitted in the first few minutes of class.
• Use a KWL chart to identify misconceptions	• Students submit K (know) and W (want to know) responses to a collaborative site where they can see each others' responses or submit their responses on a survey form for their teacher to review.	Teachers no longer have to rely on powers of persuasion to get students to raise their hand and contribute to a discussion. Now, they can make sure every student participates by giving them a digital space to submit their answer and then clarify misconceptions as soon as possible.

DURING A LESSON OR UNIT

In the first chapter of *#FormativeTech*, we discussed how important it is to check in with students during a lesson to make sure they understand the content you are teaching. This can help you focus your attention on students who need extra help and support students who have demonstrated mastery and are working independently on another task. With technology tools, teachers can use their time efficiently and strategically, making it easier to differentiate learning and meet the needs of all of their students.

A **learning management system** (LMS) is an online tool to help organize the workflow of student activities. Teachers can use an LMS to send assignments to students, provide access to a class discussion board, or to give students a place for them to submit work. Examples of an LMS: Edmodo, iTunes U, Google Classroom

There are a variety of ways teachers can leverage the power of technology to collect information during a lesson. Formative assessments can be embedded within a lesson to see if students understand a skill. If students are working on mobile devices or have one nearby, they can scan a QR code connected to a Google Form to answer a question, or log in to a learning management system and post a response to a prompt. This type of formative assessment gives teachers information on student understanding in the moment— when there is still time to intervene and support learners in the middle of a lesson.

Katrina Keene is an educator in Tennessee who uses Nearpod to embed questions into her instruction. This interactive presentation tool lets her take a slide-based presentation like PowerPoint and add questions in between the slides. With the open-ended questions she embeds in her instruction, Katrina can see in real time if her students are on track. She can pause her teaching, push out a question, and immediately see who understands the lesson and who needs extra help.

Technology tools can also be used to collect information as you circulate and move about the room. In the past, teachers might have had checklists on clipboards with scribbles or color coding to help them decide who needs help during a lesson. Instead of checking off boxes on a "*Who's got it? Checklist*" or jotting down reminders to meet with a struggling student,

A **discussion thread** is an online space for a conversation, where users comment on an initial post or the responses of others.

teachers can now log anecdotal notes in a digital platform to track student progress. This can replace traditional formative assessment practices that might have left a teacher flipping through binders or searching for sticky notes with information from a student conference. In Chapter 4, we'll talk more about customizing data collection in the workshop model as students work independently.

This example of embedded questions can help a teacher determine who in his or her class needs extra help with key concepts and vocabulary from the day's lesson.

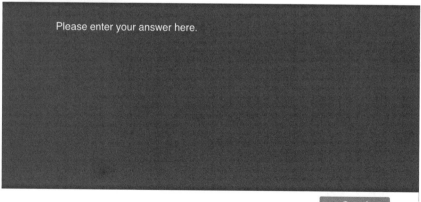

When you hear the word "biodiversity," what does it bring to mind? What does it mean?

Please enter your answer here.

Send

SOURCE: https://nearpod.com/

During a lesson, teachers can pause to send a comprehension question to students. This provides a window into student thinking when there is still time in a lesson to intervene.

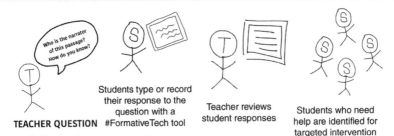

TEACHER QUESTION

5-10 seconds

Students type or record their response to the question with a #FormativeTech tool

2-3 minutes

Teacher reviews student responses

60-90 seconds

Students who need help are identified for targeted intervention

Google Form Checklist—Teachers can use an online survey tool like Google Forms to customize their data collection. This makes it possible to check for student understanding and record observations with just a few taps on the screen.

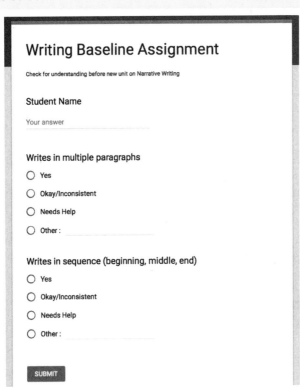

Writing Baseline Assignment

Check for understanding before new unit on Narrative Writing

Student Name

Your answer

Writes in multiple paragraphs

○ Yes

○ Okay/Inconsistent

○ Needs Help

○ Other :

Writes in sequence (beginning, middle, end)

○ Yes

○ Okay/Inconsistent

○ Needs Help

○ Other :

SUBMIT

SOURCE: www.chalkup.co

Table 2.2   During a Lesson or Unit

In a traditional classroom	In a tech-friendly classroom	Working smarter, not harder
• Confer with individual students	• Pause a lesson and send out a comprehension question to student (See page 22, top image.)	Instead of listening in to each individual student to see if he or she "got it," push a question out to students' mobile devices and have them respond with a one- or two-sentence answer. When they send it back to you, it'll be easy to see who needs extra help and who can continue working independently.
• Listen to group or partner talk	• Use a customizable online survey tool to record your observations (See page 22, bottom image.)	Submit your observations on a mobile device and watch them appear in a spreadsheet on your computer. This makes it easy to examine patterns in student progress to help you group students effectively.
• Ask students to write a question on a sticky note	• In the middle of the lesson ask each student to pause and post one wondering or question they have on a class discussion board or in the class LMS (See image on page 24.)	This is a quick way to ask students to reflect on their learning. You might ask students to post their wondering on an open discussion thread or send their question straight to you.

Discussion Thread—Students can post a question or response to a prompt on a discussion thread. Chalkup is one example of a learning management system where students can post a question or response.

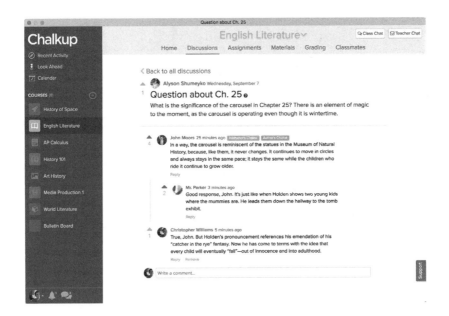

SOURCE: www.chalkup.co

AFTER A LESSON OR UNIT

When you finish a lesson, it is important to figure out how well your students understood the content you just taught. At the end of a lesson, formative assessment data collection is crucial. This is your opportunity to see if students *got it*: Do they understand the new skill or concept; are there any misconceptions? Collecting this information with technology tools makes the process more efficient and guarantees you hear from every student, not just the ones who raise their hands.

In the past, you might collect index cards with student exit slips and sort them into three groups of students with similar needs to form leveled groups for the next day's lesson. With technology tools, students can submit a short response or answer a few multiple-choice questions. You can instantly view patterns in student understanding and make decisions for whole-class and small-group instruction. This is also the time you can see if one or two students need individual intervention or enrichment. In Chapter 6, we'll take a closer look at strategies to help analyze all of the data you will collect with tech-friendly formative assessments.

Using screencasts or video reflections at the end of a lesson is a powerful way to capture student thinking. A screencast gives you a window into your students' thought process by letting you *see* and *hear* their thinking. Sometimes student explanations can become lost in translation when they compose sentences or tap an answer choice on the screen. With technology tools, teachers can ask students to create a 30-second clip summarizing their thinking. Students can now capture the steps they used to solve a math problem or answer a close-reading question.

> A **screencast** is a video recording of anything that appears on the screen of your digital device including illustrations, annotations, and voice recording. Examples of screencasting tools: Explain Everything, ShowMe, Educreations

Here are a few examples of prompts a teacher might give students before they create a screencast or video:

- *Snap a picture of the graphic organizer on your desk (or take a screenshot of your digital graphic organizer). Explain the similarities and differences between the two ecosystems you compared and contrasted with your partner today.*
- *Record a screencast showing the steps you took to solve Question #4. Explain your thinking as you move through the steps to solve this multiplication word problem.*

In addition to screencasts, video reflections are a great way for students of all ages to demonstrate their understanding. Young students can snap a picture of math manipulatives on their desk and speak about their understanding of groups of 10. Older students can explain more complex topics in words as they prepare to write explanations of

> Screencasts and video reflections are fantastic ways for English Language Learners to demonstrate their understanding. It can build confidence in students and help you understand exactly where students need extra support or enrichment.

their thinking. Students who are working on their language acquisition skills or struggle to demonstrate their understanding in writing can include the domain-specific vocabulary they might be comfortable using in a conversation—but not in a writing response—in their screencast.

So how will students get these video reflections into your hands, that is, send them to your device? The answer to this question depends on the workflow in your classroom. You might have students upload their recording to a shared cloud folder, send it to you via email, or post it on a discussion thread in your LMS. This might sound complicated, but it is truly just a few taps on the screen, depending on the workflow tools you're using in your classroom. In the next two chapters, you'll learn how to embed #FormativeTech routines like this one into your regular instruction.

> A **workflow** is the way students get work from their device to their teacher's device and vice versa.

Figuring out what number to enter into a gradebook is not the purpose of formative assessment. The purpose of formative assessment is not to simply enter a grade in a gradebook when reviewing a final or culminating project. Formative assessment data provides teachers and students with an opportunity to reflect on the learning process and set goals for future instruction and upcoming units of study.

Timely feedback is an important part of the formative assessment cycle, and technology tools make this job easier for everyone. After students submit their work electronically, teachers can open each students' submission on their own laptop or mobile device. Many learning management systems give teachers a space to comment on student work so students can see your responses automatically. Other annotation tools let teachers open up student work and add text and voice notes in addition to using a highlighter or pen tool to mark up a text. With a tap on their screen, teachers can send back notes to students instead of waiting until the next class period to pass out papers. Chapter 4 will discuss feedback routines with #Formative Tech in more detail.

Visit the companion website to learn more about a few of my favorite screencasting apps and workflow management tools. Scan the QR code at the end of this chapter to go to http://resources.corwin.com/formativetech

Screencasting—Explain Everything is a popular screencasting tool that lets students draw on their screen and record their voice. It captures thinking and gives teachers a window into each student's thought process. Students can *explain everything* from steps to follow in a science experiment to the difference between two characters in a picture book.

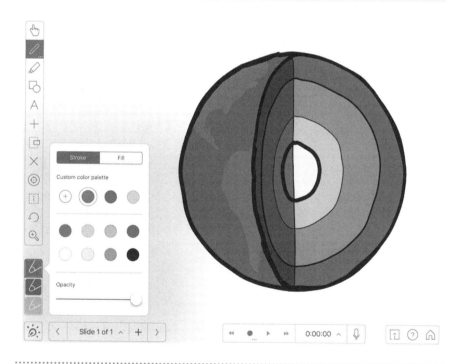

TABLE 2.3 After a Lesson or Unit

In a traditional classroom	In a tech-friendly classroom	Working smarter, not harder, with technology
• Collect an exit slip with student responses to a comprehension question	• Students submit a response to a comprehension question using their mobile device or computer.	Gathering data through technology tools makes it easier to discover patterns. Skimming a spreadsheet of short responses or using an item analysis tool can help you quickly see patterns including *who's got it* and *who needs extra help.*
• Ask students to tell you something they found confusing in a lesson	• Students record a screencast where they use their voice and drawings on a screen to explain their understanding of a concept.	Instead of asking students, "What are you struggling with?" and getting an answer that shows they *don't know what they don't know*, you can listen in to your students' thought process. A screencast captures students' moves when solving a problem or thinking through an answer.
• Review final projects to look for skill gaps that can be addressed in an upcoming unit	• Students submit their final work in any digital form to an online platform or learning management system.	Teachers can collect student work through an online platform. This means teachers can review student work and add comments without carrying a pile of papers everywhere they go. Students can review feedback as soon as the teacher posts it on the online platform.

Seesaw is a learning management system that incorporates screencasting and video recording. With this tool, students can snap a picture and talk about their learning. Children in a math class might discuss how they figured out the answer to a word problem. Students in an English Language Arts class could take a picture of the first draft of their narrative writing and discuss what revisions they made in class that day.

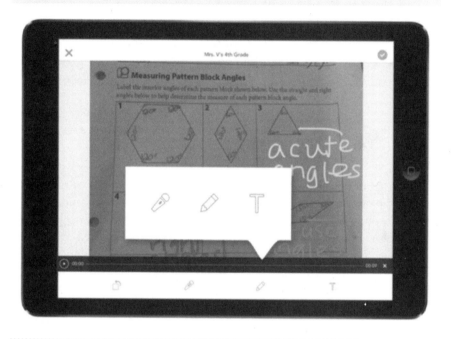

SOURCE: Seesaw

Tools for Collecting Work:

- Google Classroom: If your school is using Google Classroom, students can submit work to this platform for teachers to review. This means they can easily submit a Google Doc or Google Slides presentation to their teacher, who can leave feedback using the comments option.
- iTunes U: If your school is using iTunes U, students can submit work created in Pages, Keynote, or a range of apps straight to the iTunes U course for their class. Teachers can access and review student work by logging into their iTunes U course.

- Socrative: Teachers share the digital room number assigned to their account with their students. Students open the Socrative app or website on their device and enter the special room code assigned to the teacher. Then teachers send out an open-ended response for students to answer.
- The Answer Pad: Students log in to their account and are sent an open-ended question. When students submit their results, teachers can review their responses all in one place.

ADDRESSING TECHNOLOGY CHALLENGES

You do not need to be in a one-to-one classroom to use technology to gather information on student understanding. Although it would be ideal to have students submitting exit slips on their own devices or answer a few questions from their smartphone, this is not essential for success with #FormativeTech. In a classroom with just a few devices you might have students submit one video reflection a week as they rotate through stations. If you have access to a cart of devices twice a week, you might plan strategically for those days on your schedule. For example, on days when you do have access to devices, students can submit a digital response at the end of the lesson or take a quick survey to help you plan for next week's instruction. Even this small amount of technology integration will let you hear all of your students' voices, while saving you instructional and planning time. It doesn't take a huge investment of time or resources to feel the impact of #FormativeTech.

It doesn't take a huge investment of time or resources to feel the impact of #FormativeTech.

The benefits of using technology tools outweigh the risk of a slow wireless connection or unanticipated connectivity issues. #FormativeTech lets you collect information quicker, guarantees every student voice is heard, and makes it easier to analyze and act on student data. You can anticipate certain issues like setting up student logins for a new website ahead of time or downloading apps onto tablets before a lesson. But what if something goes *wrong*? Have a stack of index cards or sticky notes nearby for a backup in case the wireless network goes down or if your cart of tablets fails to charge overnight—there may be a day you need to go *old school*. Although it's important to acknowledge challenges that come with technology integration, interruptions come in all forms—from fire drills to phone calls. I strongly believe the increased efficiency and effectiveness technology brings to your formative assessment practice makes any hiccups completely worth it.

Later in this book, we'll talk more about establishing routines for #FormativeTech. In the next chapter, we'll explore some of my favorite quick and simple tips for integrating #Formative Tech on a small scale. As you continue to dive into each section of this book, use what you know about the foundation of formative assessment to brainstorm ways technology tools can elevate teaching and learning in your classroom.

Teachers all over the world use the screencasting tool Explain Everything to support formative assessment. In his research on screencasting and formative assessment, Dr. Reshan Richards of Teachers College, Columbia University, published findings on the ways students used screencasting with Explain Everything for formative self-assessment. When students finished recording portions of screencasts, they almost always hit rewind and listened back to themselves and watched their work. This happened across multiple disciplines and age levels, all without teacher prompting. Many students would then make corrections or completely redo their recordings. These interactions, collectively labeled "unprompted self-assessment," are made possible by the tools, but the teachers need to set the conditions like environment, opportunity, and access in order for students to make the best use of the technology (Richards & Meier, 2016).

TIPS FOR TODAY

- *Meaningful*: Decide on one part of a lesson to add a technology tool for formative assessment. How will this help you make decisions for future instruction?
- *Sustainable*: Figure out what works best for your teaching style and commit to trying out one new strategy for the next month. Can you replace your exit slip with an online discussion forum, or kick off each lesson with a quick poll? Decide what works best for your teaching style.
- *Scalable*: Find someone in your building—or a like-minded educator to connect with online—who will commit to trying out a new #FormativeTech strategy. How can you support one another as you introduce #FormativeTech into your classroom?

Scan this QR code to visit the companion website with extra resources and information on #FormativeTech:

 http://resources.corwin.com/formativetech

CHAPTER 3

Elevate Practice

Quick and Simple
Whole-Class Tips

There are many ways to get started with technology integration. Just like the first days of summer vacation, some people head straight to the diving board, and others simply dip their toe in the pool. It's perfectly fine to take a step back and assess the situation, including your comfort level, teaching style, and access to devices. All of this information will help you decide where to get started as you continue this #FormativeTech journey. If you're ready to elevate your practice with #FormativeTech, this chapter will set you up with a handful of quick and simple tips for whole-class integration of technology tools.

A first-grade teacher might have 30 children in his or her classroom. A tenth-grade teacher might meet with 150 students over the course of a day. It is nearly impossible to have a quality one-on-one conversation with each student in this tenth-grade setting, or during each content block in a first-grade classroom. Data collection with #FormativeTech can help teachers feel confident they have heard the voices of all of their students and addressed their collective and individual needs.

INCREASING EFFICIENCY

One of the reasons I'm so passionate about the use of technology in education is the way it can increase efficiency using technology tools to collect formative assessment data and plan with a purpose. #FormativeTech data collection and analysis can save you precious minutes of instructional time each day and hours of planning time each week. Setting up systems might take an investment of time at the start. However, similar to establishing routines in the beginning of the school year, it can make a huge impact for the rest of the year.

Imagine a classroom of fifth graders sitting in pairs watching a video clip on the causes of deforestation. They talk with their peers, explore an interactive map on their tablet, and examine a piece of informational text describing a particular economic challenge in a region—an issue that has led to increased deforestation. Instead of walking around and asking each student to name one cause of deforestation, you're sitting with a group of students who often have trouble with a close reading of informational text. In just a moment, you'll ask students to send you two causes of deforestation through an electronic exit slip. Today you've spent instructional time working with students, without worrying about data collection. At the end of the day, you can scroll through the responses students have sent you and identify any confusion or misconceptions from students. With this information, you can decide if the whole class needs to dive into another example, or if you'll pull a few students aside to review the content.

In this scenario, classroom teachers are using their time wisely. They can spend extra time with students who have demonstrated a need for an intervention instead of walking around the classroom with a checklist. Teachers can feel confident they've checked for each student's understanding by ending the lesson with an exit slip. And they'll save time reviewing student responses by quickly scanning through an electronic platform—on their smartphone, tablet, or web browser—saving time during afterschool hours to tweak the next day's lesson or plan for differentiated instruction.

Differentiated instruction is the practice of choosing resources or designing learning activities to address the needs of individual students. In this learning environment educators adjust their teaching in response to observations, and the information they have gathered, on student needs.

In the next few sections, we'll breakdown the big ideas introduced in Chapter 2. Technology tools make it easier to check for understanding and gauge student interest through polling, workflows can be customized to your teaching style and course content, and scannables can be used to quickly collect information. Keep an eye out for teacher stories, favorite tools, and best practices to apply to any type of #FormativeTech tool you integrate into your classroom instruction.

STUDENT POLLING

A quick interest survey can help you choose a direction for your lesson. It gives you a better understanding of how to introduce a new topic or make connections to real-world examples. A poll is one of my favorite formative assessment tools because it provides teachers with a lot of actionable information, even though there are no right answers.

Just like any type of technology in this book, you'll see examples of where the same tool is used for a different purpose. I call this *tasks before apps,* which you can learn more about here: classtechtips.com/tasksbeforeapps.

When conducting a poll with a technology tool, teachers have a few decisions to make. You might want to see individual student responses to plan for differentiated instruction, or you might want to examine results from the whole class to make general instructional decisions. This decision will depend on whether your purpose of polling is to get a snapshot of general student understanding to determine whole-class instruction, or gather information you can use for targeted instruction in strategic groups.

Stephanie Castle is an Apple Distinguished Educator and IB biology teacher. She uses Kahoot as a survey tool to check for student understanding. Stephanie has taken this engaging polling platform to the next level by using it as a way to introduce new concepts to students in the form of a "blind kahoot." In Stephanie's classroom, she is able to use this tool to monitor student understanding while introducing new information to students at the same time.

Kahoot is a polling tool that lets teachers create their own surveys. Students can respond to questions on their mobile device.

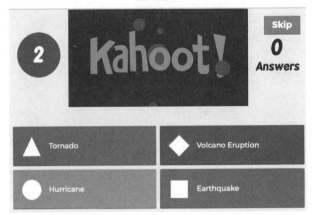

SOURCE: Kahoot

Nearpod Poll—A poll can provide useful information on student interest and understanding. Students can share their interests or prior knowledge by answering a quick poll question. This information can help teachers direct their lesson.

SOURCE: Nearpod

Table 3.1

Type of Poll	Purpose	Classroom Example	Action
Interest Survey	To make connections to subtopics students are interested in learning more about	Before kicking off a unit on national symbols, ask students: What landmark would you like to visit the most? What part of the country would you like to travel to?	If students answer *Mt. Rushmore* or *California,* you can use these examples in your discussion to grab their attention.
Misconception Check	To clarify any incorrect information that will get in the way of content mastery	As you get ready to introduce a unit on endangered species, ask students: How does an animal become endangered? What has to happen for an animal to be added to the endangered species list?	If students answer, *All animals are endangered* or *Every endangered species lives in a zoo,* you can address these misconceptions in your lesson.
Prior Knowledge	To establish a baseline of what students currently understand about a topic to plan lessons that leverage what they already know	On the first day of a unit on fractions, ask students to choose the correct definition for the following terms: *improper fraction, mixed number, ratio.*	If the majority of students already know these terms, you won't have to dedicate time to review vocabulary.
Past Experiences	To avoid repeating experiences students have already had when exploring this topic in the past	As you get ready to introduce a unit on the Civil War, ask students which books or movies on this list they have already read or watched: *Pink and Say, The Red Badge of Courage, Gone with the Wind, Cold Mountain.*	If most students have never read the book *Pink and Say,* you might decide to begin your unit by reading this book aloud to students.

Another factor to consider when conducting a poll with technology tools is if and how you will share whole-class results. Some tools let you display student responses on a projector screen for students, others let you collect data from individual students, and many do both. How to tackle this issue really comes down to how you plan to use this formative assessment data—and there might be more than one answer. If you are conducting a poll to check for misconceptions, you won't want to call out individual students in front of the whole class. However, you may want to display the results of a poll to the whole class and have a conversation that addresses some of the interests or prior knowledge visible in poll results.

Polls can also be used to form groups in your class. Instead of creating a group in your ecology classroom of students who like the same sport, use interest surveys to form groups of students who are interested in exploring the same subtopics in your next unit. For example, ask students to respond to questions to gauge their interest about different biomes and use this information to create groups that will investigate each one. Students who indicate their preference for a *toucan* over a *humpback whale* could be more engaged in a group studying the rainforest than in one studying the ocean. The purpose of formative assessment data collection is to give you information to inform your decisions—from grouping students to the structure of your lesson. With #FormativeTech, you can collect this data quickly and share student responses with your class anonymously.

REPLACE THE CLIPBOARD

When we think of formative assessment in traditional classrooms, you might imagine the following: a teacher pacing around a classroom, hands grasping a clipboard, while peeking over the shoulders of students solving math problems on a worksheet. Then the teacher places a checkmark next to the name of students who have written correct answers and an *x* next to students who struggle. Maybe this teacher takes the clipboard back to his or her desk and calls over the six

Poll Everywhere—Teachers can launch a poll for students to learn about their interests. Students can respond using a text message on their smartphone or enter a response into a web browser. This tool is perfect for polling students or groups every once and awhile since it doesn't require users to login.

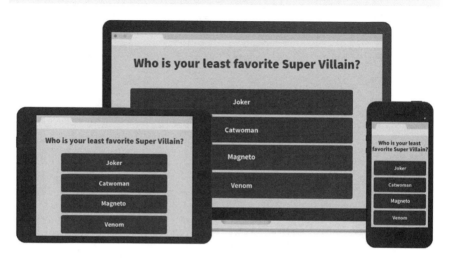

SOURCE: Poll Everywhere

students who are struggling with a particular math problem to help them complete the assignment with a new strategy. Maybe later in the month, the teacher looks over the pages on the clipboard and sees two students in particular have been struggling for the past few weeks. Now they know that a more strategic intervention needs to be developed to meet the needs of those students.

In a classroom using #FormativeTech, teachers can use digital checklist or replace this practice completely. This digital checklists strategy is perfect for teachers with access to just one device. As students work on pencil and paper, teachers can use their mobile device to gather data more effectively. Using a portable tablet with a touchscreen, teachers can move about the room and tap on their screen to enter data. There are a variety of tools that let teachers create customizable data entry forms, and I've had a lot of success using Google Forms for this purpose.

Plickers—Teachers in low-tech classrooms can use the tool Plickers to gather quick formative assessment data. With Plickers, each student is given a set of response cards that represent different answers to a multiple-choice or yes/no question. The students can hold up their cards while the teacher scans the room with his or her tablet or smartphone, instantly collecting student data.

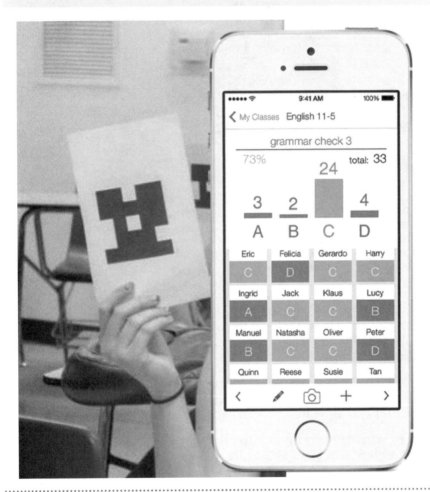

SOURCE: Plickers

As an elementary school teacher instructing students in all subject areas, Google Forms were especially useful for replacing clipboards and paper checklists in my classroom. As a collaborative team teacher, it was also a game changer for data collection. Google Forms are a customizable data entry form so users can create their own survey-like form to collect information, like data on student understanding. If you haven't used them in your classroom, you've probably filled one out to submit information for a conference or a potluck dinner. I created a handful of Google Forms to make it easy to enter information about individual student performance, similar to a checklist. Any information I entered into the form automatically went to a spreadsheet hosted in my Google Drive. Both my co-teacher and I could submit data into the same form on our individual iPad, and the results would appear in a spreadsheet. It was an easy way to combine our data collection efforts and view patterns in our class of fifth graders as we checked for understanding.

One-to-one refers to classrooms where each student has his or her own device like an iPad or Chromebook. This device was most likely provided by the school and is the same type of device as everyone else in their class. **BYOD** or **bring your own device** refers to settings where students are allowed to bring in their own technology tool from home, such as a smartphone, tablet, or laptop. This creates a classroom environment with a mix of devices.

Using a Checklist

Teacher observes students working and enters notes into a digital checklist

Teacher reviews observations from the day or week

Teacher works with students who need extra help or enrichment

This Google Form checklist is set up to collect observations on student mastery during a math lesson.

Math Checklist

Learning Objective

Student Mastery

	Got it!	Working on it	Needs Help	Absent
Joey	○	○	○	○
Rachel	○	○	○	○
Ross	○	○	○	○
Monica	○	○	○	○
Chandler	○	○	○	○

Extra Notes

Submit

The responses submitted to the Google Form above automatically appear in Google Sheet, making it easier for teachers to organize and share formative assessment data.

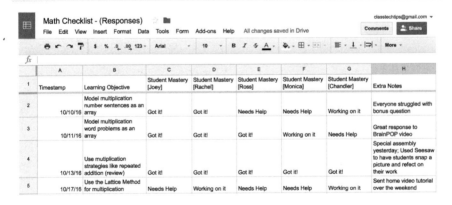

	A	B	C	D	E	F	G	H
1	Timestamp	Learning Objective	Student Mastery [Joey]	Student Mastery [Rachel]	Student Mastery [Ross]	Student Mastery [Monica]	Student Mastery [Chandler]	Extra Notes
2	10/10/16	Model multiplication number sentences as an array	Got it!	Got it!	Needs Help	Needs Help	Working on it	Everyone struggled with bonus question
3	10/11/16	Model multiplication word problems as an array	Got it!	Got it!	Got it!	Working on it	Needs Help	Great response to BrainPOP video
4	10/13/16	Use mutiplication strategies like repeated addition (review)	Got it!	Got it!	Got it!	Got it!	Got it!	Special assembly yesterday; Used Seesaw to have students snap a picture and refect on their work
5	10/17/16	Use the Lattice Method for multiplication	Needs Help	Working on it	Needs Help	Needs Help	Working on it	Sent home video tutorial over the weekend

Table 3.2

Type of Checklist	Purpose	Classroom Example
Daily objectives	To see if students understand the learning target for the day's lesson	As students work in pairs to solve a math word problem with multidigit multiplication, the teacher circulates around the room, listening in to student conversations and taking note of each student's level of mastery.
Weekly goals	To see if students have mastered the skill(s) you are working on during a short period of time	Over the course of a week, the teacher checks in with students during individual or group conversations or through observations to see if they are able to compare and contrast two characters from their independent reading book.
Anecdotal notes	To collect more information on student understanding in the form of a sentence (not a yes/no response)	When meeting with students, listening in to conversations or reviewing student work, the teacher jots down notable information to help future groupings, interventions, and whole-class instructional goals, such as *Maria struggled to retell a story in sequence.*

At Ossining High School in New York, English teacher Adam Schoenbart uses Google Forms to assess student understanding quickly and efficiently. Adam creates Google Forms for students to submit answers to questions to check for understanding. If students enter incorrect answers to multiple choice activities on a Google Form, the responses are automatically analyzed to show areas where students need extra support. This provides important data for re-teaching in whole-class and small-group instruction. The same kind of strategy can be adapted for *exit ticket* or *do now* activities at the beginning of class.

If you're working in a one-to-one classroom or BYOD (bring your own device) learning environment you have more options for getting rid of paper checklists. Teachers can replace checklists completely by asking students to submit answers to a few questions electronically. These are the same questions you might include on an activity sheet or an assignment teachers might look at when peeking over student shoulders while holding a clipboard. Instead of teachers marking down whether each student *got it* or not, students can submit their own answers with a few taps on the screen. Teachers can worry less about collecting data and more about acting on information they've already received from formative assessment data in previous lessons.

CHOOSE A SYSTEM

As you get ready to integrate #FormativeTech into whole-class lessons, step back for a moment to examine your goals. In addition to identifying the purpose for using formative assessments to gather information on student needs, you'll want to determine how different types of technology tools can support this mission. There are a variety of tools designed to help teachers create easy workflow systems. A workflow is a means of communication, a process that takes place between you (and your device) and your students (and their mobile device or computer).

Table 3.3

Type of Workflows	Purpose	Classroom Example
Send a response	To get a quick check of student understanding through a response to a question or prompt	At the end of a lesson on the rock cycle, ask students to send an answer to the question, *What is the difference between metamorphic and sedimentary rocks?*
Submit a document	To examine any document students are working on, such as a PDF, video recording, or collaborative slide deck	Ask students to submit the first draft of their personal narrative so you can add a few comments for them to review.
Comment on a discussion thread	To check student understanding through an authentic response in a space open to the entire class	Have students open up your class LMS (learning management system) to post a comment on the discussion thread you started for today's lesson on determining the theme of a science fiction passage.
Answer multiple-choice questions	To check student understanding quickly	Share the link to a set of multiple-choice questions related to the day's lesson on Spanish verb tenses.

Digital citizenship refers to the way students use technology in an appropriate manner including responsible online interactions and citation of resources found online. To learn more about digital citizenship, explore *Digital Citizenship: A Community-Based Approach* by Susan Bearden.

A discussion thread provides an opportunity for an authentic response to content. At the same time, it addresses the goal of gathering formative assessment data and provides a space for students to develop digital citizenship skills. Commenting in open, social spaces is a skill students need in the real world. You might use a discussion

Commenting Anchor Chart—Erica Shepherd is a fourth-grade teacher in Louisiana. She posts an anchor chart to remind her students of the expectations for leaving comments on the blog posts of fellow students.

SOURCE: Erica Shepherd

board in a lesson every once and awhile, or use discussion boards as a regular routine in your classroom.

You might want to provide a few simple guidelines to aid students in commenting and posting on a discussion board. For example:

Comments should

- Address the task
- Be relevant to our work
- Be concise and clear
- Be supportive and productive

Authentic learning experiences connect student activities to the real world. Designing experiences that are relevant to students and related to their everyday lives is an important part of demonstrating the purpose of the learning taking place in school.

SUBMITTING WITH SCANNABLES

Scannable technology can be used to help students submit responses quickly and easily. QR codes can take students to online spaces where they can submit formative assessment data. If you haven't scanned a QR code, you've probably seen them on advertisements or at a conference—they're also spread throughout this book. A QR code is easy to make; just copy and paste the link you want students to access into a QR code generator then share the QR code you've made with students. Students can scan the QR code with a QR code scanning app on any mobile device with a wireless connection or cellular signal.

Use QRstuff.com to make QR codes and try the mobile app i-nigma to scan QR codes. Visit the companion site for links to these resources. http://resources.corwin.com/formativetech

Teacher creates an online survey and turns the link into a QR code

Students scan the QR code

Students answer the questions on the online survey

Teacher reviews student responses

Maggie Padua is a fourth-grade teacher at Learners and Leaders Academy in New York City. She's used a QR code to make it easy for students to submit answers to reading comprehension questions. When you walk into her classroom, you can see students holding up their iPad to scan a QR code projected on the board in the front of the room. When students scan this QR code, they are immediately taken to a Google Form to record their learning at the end of class, a virtual exit slip with responses Maggie can easily review in her Google Drive.

Since a QR code connects to any website you choose, teachers use it as a way for students to submit their work or access a collaborative space. For example, students can scan a QR code you've connected to a survey tool like Google Forms to submit a response to a question. Students could also scan a QR code to take them to a collaborative board like Padlet, where they can add a virtual sticky note to a webpage as an exit slip.

Using an LMS like iTunes U or Google Classroom gives students instant access to any link you post. Of course, it is wonderful to lead a lesson in a one-to-one classroom where all students access the same learning management system every day. Scannable technology is a great option for classrooms without a predetermined LMS to post links for students. Scannable technology makes it easy for students to quickly get to a website where they can submit a response to their teacher. QR codes also work well in BYOD classrooms where students have access to a variety of environments.

The words *quick, quickly,* and *efficient* were used 18 times in this chapter. #FormativeTech helps teachers save instructional time by collecting data on student understanding. Students can spend more minutes exploring content during the learning journey in your classroom instead of showing you what they know. We'll continue to discuss the importance of working smarter, not harder, as we move through the next few chapters. As we get started on our #FormativeTech journey, think of all the minutes you can save each school day with these quick and simple whole-class tips.

Scannable technology is the interaction of mobile devices and a trigger image to connect users to content. This can include QR codes or augmented reality. Interested in learning more about scannable technology? Take a look at *Deeper Learning with QR Codes and Augmented Reality: A Scannable Solution for Your Classroom.* **QR CODE LINK classtechtips .com/books**

TIPS FOR TODAY

- *Meaningful*: Choose one type of poll to kick off a lesson. How will you use the information you receive to form groups or direct your lesson?
- *Sustainable*: Explore one of the workflow options (i.e., send a response, submit a document, comment on a discussion thread, answer multiple-choice questions) for gathering student responses. Try out this option with your class over the course of the week. Does this option match your teaching style and give you actionable data?
- *Scalable*: Share your experience gathering formative assessment data with technology at a grade-level team meeting or faculty gathering. Ask other teachers to share their tips for collecting formative assessment data. How can you support other staff members in your school or use their tips in your classroom?

Scan this QR code to visit the companion website with extra resources and information on #FormativeTech:

 http://resources.corwin.com/formativetech

CHAPTER 4

Using #FormativeTech With Independent Learners

Independent practice is an essential component of a lesson. After introducing a topic or modelling a strategy, students need time to apply what they've learned. #FormativeTech can be used in many settings to gather information on student understanding. In the beginning of this book, we discussed how technology tools could be used before, during, and after a lesson to figure out how well students have mastered content. When students are working independently or in small groups, teachers want to make sure they understand the new skill or topic they have introduced.

Picture your students hard at work. They might be tackling a tough math word problem with a classmate or discussing the most recent chapter they've read in *Walk Two Moons* during a literature circle. You might find students working their way through an independent research project on a European nation or measuring the growth of a bean plant with a lab partner. Although the goals of students are different in each of these scenarios, your goal as a teacher remains the same. Teachers support, monitor, and facilitate independent learning in their classroom after modeling a skill or introducing a topic.

SUPPORTING INDEPENDENT LEARNERS

In a workshop model, you might use the phrase *I do, we do, you do* to describe the gradual release of learning during a lesson. A first-grade classroom might kick off with a mini-lesson on generating writing ideas for an *All About Me* book. Students watch as the teacher models how to list ideas (*I do*), then students talk together about their own ideas (*we do*). After the mini-lesson, students are set off to work on their own list of ideas for their personal *All About Me* book (*you do*).

> The gradual release of responsibility model shifts the heavy lifting of the lesson from the teacher to student. The teacher might start off modelling a skill, but strategically provides opportunities for students to become independent (Pearson & Gallagher, 1983).

In a ninth-grade classroom, a teacher might introduce a timeline of events for the Vietnam War (*I do*), then students work together to investigate an area of the timeline (*we do*). At the end of the lesson, students are asked to describe a significant moment in the conflict using

I Do, We Do, You Do

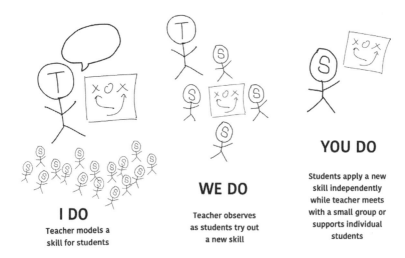

I DO
Teacher models a skill for students

WE DO
Teacher observes as students try out a new skill

YOU DO
Students apply a new skill independently while teacher meets with a small group or supports individual students

what they've learned in their partner discovery and teacher-led mini-lesson (*you do*).

When students are sent off in pairs or asked to work independently, there is a clear purpose for learning. You have released them from the grip of teacher talk to explore content and apply what they've learned. During this time, a teacher might work with a small group of students to help them strengthen a skill or strategy. Alternatively, a teacher might sit next to a student who requires one-on-one support to transfer what they've learned to their individual work. It is essential that there are clear systems for checking in and monitoring student progress while students work independently. Collecting formative assessment data during this time will help teachers figure out who requires extra help, who has mastered content, and how to frame whole- and small-group instruction in the days and weeks moving forward. #FormativeTech helps teachers collect meaningful data on student understanding in an efficient manner.

SYSTEMS FOR CHECKING IN

In addition to the quick and simple tips mentioned in the previous chapter, developing *regular systems* with #FormativeTech can help teachers remain confident that all students receive the instructional support they need. #FormativeTech can help teachers check-in on individual student progress during independent practice time. Technology tools simplify the process of collecting formative assessment data. Whether students are working in small groups, pairs, or independently, #FormativeTech can make the task of collecting information on student progress easier and efficient. Teachers can take the minutes they save using technology tools for data collection and increase instructional time with students who need strategic intervention, enrichment, or extra support.

> An **interactive response tool** lets students annotate an image sent to their device by a teacher or submit an answer through text and/or drawing. Examples: TheAnswerPad, Socrative, Nearpod

Earlier in this book, we examined how *do nows* or *exit slips* are options for formative assessment in both traditional and tech-infused classrooms. These are two examples of ways teachers can check student understanding on a daily or weekly basis. In this section, we will look at the ways a teacher can check for student understanding when students have spent time working independently—both during and at the end of a lesson. Although there are a variety of tools to choose from, the illustrations in this chapter are designed to help you imagine the workflow you can bring into your classroom regardless of the tool you choose. The work-flow examples are designed for teachers looking to gather information on student understanding, while children are working independently in a workshop model (*I do, we do, you do*), or when students are sent to work independently during a lesson.

Nili Bartley is an educator from Hopkinton, Massachusetts. She uses the quiz tool built into BrainPOP to check for student understanding. BrainPOP contains videos that provide explanations on topics like Carbon Dating and Ocean Currents. This website and mobile app has quizzes, graphic organizers, and lesson materials for teachers. Nili uses quizzes in BrainPOP to see where students struggle when exploring new content. After looking at the information she's received at the end of a quiz, Nili can target her instruction to meet the needs of the children in her class.

A *mid-lesson check* is designed to interrupt independent practice. Imagine you are teaching a lesson to sixth graders on how to identify anachronisms in historical fiction. Once students are halfway through the time allocated for independent practice, the teacher can pause independent work to get the class's attention. A mid-lesson check might ask students to write a one-sentence response to the question, *What anachronism did you find during your reading of the short passage today?* Students can submit their response to a learning management system or through a survey tool. The teacher can skim through responses as students go back to work and then gather the students who need extra help before the bell rings.

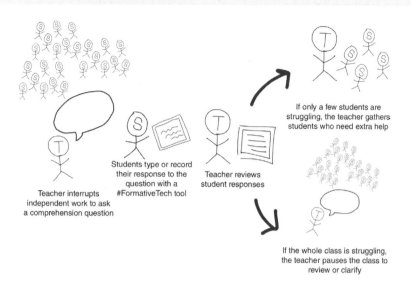

Teacher interrupts independent work to ask a comprehension question

Students type or record their response to the question with a #FormativeTech tool

Teacher reviews student responses

If only a few students are struggling, the teacher gathers students who need extra help

If the whole class is struggling, the teacher pauses the class to review or clarify

A mid-lesson check-in could also give students an opportunity to ask for help. Students using an interactive response tool can indicate how confident they are as they work through the lesson. There might also be a space for them to post a question when they are confused. Imagine you are working with a small group of students and have encouraged other children in your class not to interrupt your small-group session. The students know they can still send a question to you if they are struggling.

When introducing a new concept to your class, you want to know if every student understood what has been taught. An *activity check* with #Formative Tech provides a glimpse into student progress. In a first-grade

Joe Romano is a Library Media Specialist in Tacoma, Washington. He uses the ActivelyLearn platform's embedded questions as a way to check for understanding. His students are able to read a piece of text and highlight different lines as they document their thinking. Joe can quickly review their annotations, offer feedback, and make sure all of his students understand the concepts he's teaching.

classroom, students might work with math manipulatives on their desk to form rectangular arrays. An activity check with #FormativeTech might include asking students to snap a picture of one of their arrays with a tablet and record their voice explaining what the manipulatives represent. In a tenth-grade science classroom, students might send their teacher a link to a collaborative document to show what they've added to their lab report during class time.

Learning to reflect purposefully is an essential real-world skill.

This type of submission might not happen on a daily basis, but frequently enough for you to feel confident you are monitoring the progress of each individual student. The information you gather from an activity check can help you form groups of students who have similar needs so you can provide strategic instruction. It also helps teachers understand what part of their future plans should be modified to meet the needs of the whole class.

Illustrated Workflow for an Activity Check

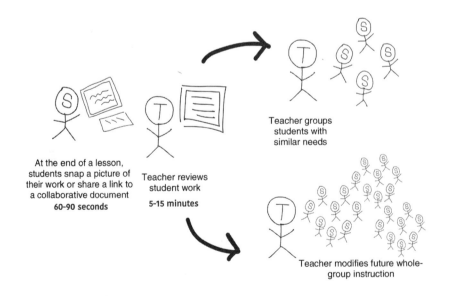

At the end of a lesson, students snap a picture of their work or share a link to a collaborative document
60-90 seconds

Teacher reviews student work
5-15 minutes

Teacher groups students with similar needs

Teacher modifies future whole-group instruction

#FORMATIVETECH

A student reflection is a powerful piece of formative assessment data. Students should be asked to periodically reflect on their progress and identify areas they need help in. Learning to reflect purposefully is an essential real-world skill. Reflections also give teachers a window into student thinking and provide information on areas where students need support. It gives teachers information on how students are feeling and what they are thinking about a project.

For example, in a kindergarten classroom, students might use the camera on their tablet to record a video where they talk about what they learned from a read aloud. In a seventh-grade classroom, students might create a screencast where they annotate an image of their work and make a plan for revisions during the next class period. Chapter 5 will include a discussion on reflections with #FormativeTech in the context of long-term projects. You can tailor these tips to everyday activities.

Drawp for School is a tool teachers can use to make student work submission seamless. It puts tools in the hands of students so they can show their understanding. This includes an audio tool that is perfect for capturing reflections.

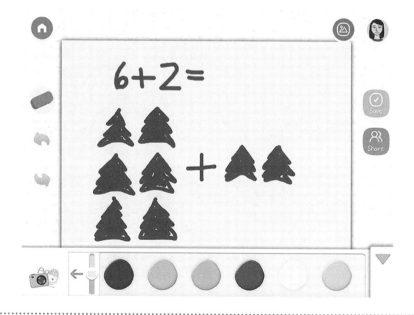

SOURCE: Drawp for School

Table 4.1   Regular Check-Ins (daily, weekly)

Type	What does this looks like?	How could you use this data?
Mid-lesson	The teacher poses a question to the class in the *middle* of a lesson while students are working independently.	Students submit a response to a question through an interactive response tool—just a sentence or two. Teachers can skim the responses they receive as students return to their independent work. If the teacher sees that a few students are struggling, they can check in with them in a small group. If all students are struggling, they can pause the class to review a concept or clarify an idea.
Activity	Students are asked to submit the activity they worked on during independent practice time (completed or in progress) at the *end* of class.	Students submit the activity they worked on during class by sharing a link to their document, snapping a picture, and sending a progress update through an interactive response tool. The teacher reviews student submissions and now has a sense of student understanding after examining their work.
Reflection	Students reflect on what they have accomplished during the day's lesson at the *end* of class.	Students submit a reflection through an interactive response tool. This could include a video reflection, a screencast recording, or a short written message. Teachers can then review student reflections and tweak instructional goals for the next set of lessons based on their observations.

ACTIONABLE FEEDBACK

Have you ever received an assignment back from a teacher or professor and only seen a number grade? What does a grade of 95, 85, or 75 really tell a student? Formative assessment is not about a number grade. *Feedback* can enhance the learning experience of students by providing information that addresses strengths, areas of need, and/or misconceptions. Feedback makes the cycle of formative assessment more transparent for teachers and students, as well as any other educators providing support to that child.

Teachers should not feel the need to provide feedback on every piece of student work, in every subject area, every day. Not only is this an unreasonable request to place on teachers, it would be overwhelming for students to sort through mounds of feedback on their work. Teachers should choose the pieces of student work requiring feedback strategically. For example, you might choose to leave a few comments on every student's document halfway through a unit where students are writing an English Language Arts research project on endangered species. For some students, you might

Lisa Dabel is an elementary school teacher in Cupertino Union School District, California. She uses the interactive tool Drawp for School with her students to check for understanding. In Lisa's classroom she can send out activities for students using Drawp for School and the children in her classroom can record their voice as part of their response. The recordings students make with Drawp for School provide a window into student thinking that shows Lisa whether or not her students understand a concept.

At the Philadelphia Performing Arts Charter School, the high school English Department uses iPads to check for student understanding. One particular assignment is a formative assessment about using the rhetorical devices of *logos*, *ethos*, and *pathos* (i.e., how factual information, a speaker's credibility, and the emotional appeal to the audience, respectively, work together to persuade, inform, or entertain). Students are asked to write their own small speech of about four to five sentences and create an audio recording using the app Spark Video. Teachers can then review student videos to check for understanding and make a plan for future instruction.

decide to check in more frequently and alert them to be on the lookout for your feedback during the writing process. As you review student work and provide feedback to students, you are on a formative assessment fact-finding mission. The observations you make will help you figure out how to help students on their learning journey, while building their accountability as independent learners.

Feedback should be timely, relevant, and actionable:

- *Timely:* Students see your feedback a day or two after they've submitted work, with more time allotted for longer tasks.
- *Relevant:* Students see the point in your feedback, and they understand how it relates to what they are working on.
- *Actionable:* Students can use the information as a next step, to complete an action the teacher has clearly identified in their suggestions.

A star, sticker, or smiley face is not feedback—it is an acknowledgement or encouragement. It does not provide students with information on how they can improve as they work toward mastering content. Feedback should be simple enough for students to understand what

> Feedback should be timely, relevant, and actionable.

Table 4.2 Feedback Examples

Grade	Topic	What strong feedback should look like . . .
First	Narrative writing	*I like the way you included details about your characters' feelings. Try adding a few pieces of dialogue so your reader knows what your characters were talking about during their trip to the beach.*
Fifth	Geometry	*You did a great job including labels on your graph. Next time, make sure to include domain-specific vocabulary in your explanation.*
Tenth	European history	*The draft of your research report includes a clear introduction and thesis statement. If you take a look at Chapter 17 in our textbook, you can find key details to support your argument.*

they have to do next to deepen their understanding of a topic or apply a new skill correctly.

The examples in Table 4.2 demonstrate relevant and actionable feedback—it's related to the task and gives students a next step. It is essential that students also receive feedback in a timely manner. If you are asking students to add something to their story, the feedback should arrive in time for them to make a change. If you notice you are giving the same feedback to a few students and you do so in a timely and consistent manner, you will have time to create a strategy group of students who

Nikki Vradenburg is an educator from Montana who works with kindergarten and first graders. She has her students watch BrainPOP videos and summarize what they've learned in a screencast. The students then post their video summaries on their personal EasyBlog so Nikki can listen to her students' thinking and comment on their post. One of her students expressed interest in learning more about colloids after watching a BrainPOP video on states of matter. Nikki used this information when she met with the student to help them dive deeper into the topic.

Kaizena is a tool that lets teachers add written or audio feedback to work students have submitted digitally.

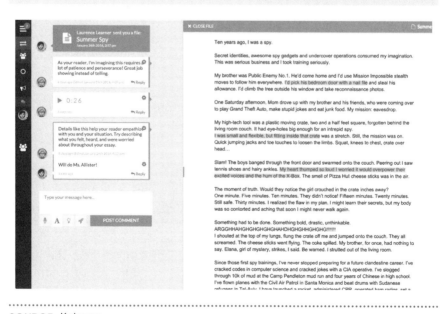

SOURCE: Kaizena

Stephanie Trautman is a middle school English teacher and writer for Common Sense Media who uses Kaizena to give feedback to her students. She attaches voice messages to student digital work to offer guidance to her students. One of her favorite features is the comment feature, where she can prefabricate comments for each class and then attach them to student work. The comments can include a thoughtful remark and then a link for students to visit in order to find out more about a topic.

have the same needs before you move on to a new topic. We'll talk more about strategy groups as an intervention for struggling students in Chapter 6.

#FormativeTech makes it easier to give students feedback in a timely manner. If you are collecting student work digitally, you can post a comment on their work, and they'll see your response in real time. Many technology tools give teachers the option to add voice notes to their students' work. This can save teachers time by giving them the opportunity to record feedback as opposed to sending an email or writing feedback on a sticky note.

BACKCHANNELS IN K–12

An important part of an educator's role is to make sure content and activities are relevant to learners. This doesn't mean you have to force connections in a Social Studies lesson to the most popular television show of the moment. However, you can take some of the best parts of the digital lives students lead outside of school to energize your lessons and create authentic learning experiences.

A whisper in class might be off topic, but more often than not, I've found these murmurs during a lesson are sounds of students asking a question or making a comment about what's happening in class. You can learn a lot about students—and the success of a lesson—from your students' casual conversations. A *backchannel* is an online space where students can add comments and contribute their thoughts. Backchannels provide a fantastic way to capture student thinking, encourage participation, and hold students accountable for their contributions. Teachers are collecting formative assessment data at the same time as they check for student understanding.

In Chapter 3, we examined discussion threads as a way to have students record what they've learned during a lesson. These types of comments give students a space to share and teachers an opportunity to check for understanding. A backchannel is different; it is a flowing discussion happening in real time. Student responses are in chronological order and students can view their peers' contributions as they pop up on the screen.

You can think of a backchannel like a Twitter feed during the Super Bowl halftime show. Students use a backchannel to comment as they watch a video clip or listen to a discussion

Tammy Musiowsky is an elementary school teacher in Singapore. She uses the commenting feature of Google Docs to share feedback with her students. When her second graders are writing on their Chromebooks, Tammy can peek at their work and leave a comment and next step. Students automatically receive an email message to notify them that Tammy has commented on their work. Using digital tools in this manner makes it easier for Tammy to check in frequently with students and provide timely feedback.

You can learn a lot about students—and the success of a lesson—from your students' casual conversations.

take place. Although there is a handful of platforms to choose from, some high school teachers do use Twitter as a backchannel, and each class has a hashtag to use in their tweets about class content. With a backchannel, teachers are able to view a stream of student questions and responses in real time. This gives you a sense of misconceptions or questions in the class so you can shift a discussion in the right direction. It also gives you an opportunity to pull up a backchannel after class and scroll through student responses to make decisions about future lessons.

Table 4.3   Backchannels in K-12

Type	Instruction to Students	What You'll See	What This Tells You
Open (Image A)	Comment on what you heard in today's discussion or video clip.	Students' thoughts on what they experienced in class	General observations including what information has grabbed students' attention or what misconceptions are present
Prompt (Image B)	Respond to the following question or statement.	Student responses to the prompt you've given	Which students understand content or need extra help
Question Collection (Image C)	Record any questions you have during today's discussion or at the end of class.	Student questions and wonderings	Areas students need clarification because they are confused; areas to explore in upcoming lessons because students are curious about a particular aspect of the topic

ABC   TodaysMeet

Image A: In this *open* backchannel, students post comments while watching a video on the rock cycle (Grade 4).

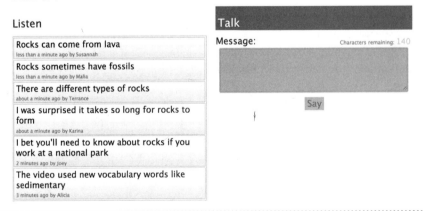

TodaysMeet

MsBPer4

Listen

Rocks can come from lava
less than a minute ago by Susannah

Rocks sometimes have fossils
less than a minute ago by Malia

There are different types of rocks
about a minute ago by Terrance

I was surprised it takes so long for rocks to form
about a minute ago by Karina

I bet you'll need to know about rocks if you work at a national park
2 minutes ago by Joey

The video used new vocabulary words like sedimentary
3 minutes ago by Alicia

Talk

Message: Characters remaining: 140

Say

SOURCE: https://todaysmeet.com/

#FORMATIVETECH

Image B: In this *prompt* backchannel, students post adjectives to describe characters in a read-aloud book (Grade 1).

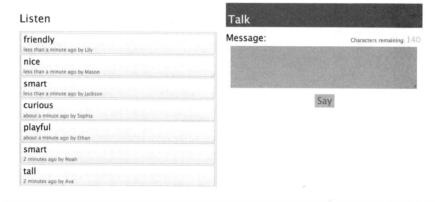

SOURCE: https://todaysmeet.com/

Image C: In this *question collection* backchannel, students post questions during a discussion of the Revolutionary War (Grade 8).

SOURCE: https://todaysmeet.com/

TJ Neville is a Middle School Social Studies educator and Google Certified Teacher from Connecticut. During each unit of study, TJ's students were constantly coming up with insightful questions. TJ created a backchannel on Padlet and encouraged his students to add their questions. Students were able to post questions and also answer the questions of their classmates. This not only created a valuable resource for the class, but also gave TJ a window into his students' thinking during the unit.

A backchannel can provide teachers with information to help them make instructional decisions during and after a lesson. You might peek at the backchannel periodically over a 40-minute block and meet with students who need help during the class period. Alternatively, you could review the backchannel at the end of a lesson and figure out if there are any concepts you need to review or misconceptions to clarify during future instruction.

When introducing backchannels to students, it is important to be clear about your expectations. A great way to set students up for success is to take time to share exemplars and nonexemplars. You can lead students in a discussion of what to do and what not to do in an open forum like a backchannel. Similar to the discussion threads mentioned in Chapter 3, set students up for success by having a digital citizenship discussion before getting started. Take time to discuss best practices for participating in a backchannel. Sharing resources like an anchor chart can help eliminate potential issues for getting started.

When teachers release students from the grips of direct instruction to apply what they learn, #FormativeTech can be used to monitor student progress. Technology tools give teachers the power to hear from every student, not the select few who raise their hand to share. Integrating quick check-ins into the time allocated for independent work provides information to shape future instructional goals. Thoughtful, actionable feedback delivered to students in a timely manner

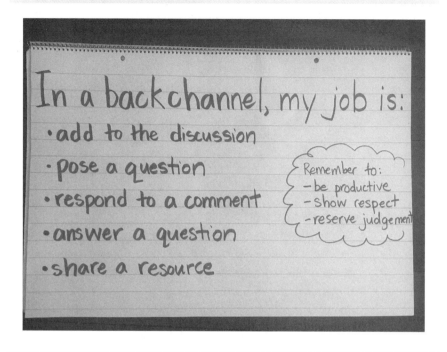

can help learners stay focused during independent, partner, and small-group time. #FormativeTech helps teachers check for understanding in more efficiently and consistently while providing richer, more meaningful data.

TIPS FOR TODAY

- *Meaningful*: Build time at the end of a lesson for students to submit the activity they completed. Provide a few options including text, picture, and video. How easily are students able to talk about their learning? What are you looking for students to show as you check for understanding?
- *Sustainable*: Choose one type of backchannel (open, prompt, question collection) to try with students. Explain the purpose and expectations to students. How can you use a backchannel once a month or once a week in your classroom?
- *Scalable*: Meet with colleagues on your grade level to discuss the feedback you give students. Lead a discussion with fellow teachers about the #FormativeTech systems to put in place so feedback on student work is timely and actionable.

Scan this QR code to visit the companion website with extra resources and information on #FormativeTech:

 http://resources.corwin.com/formativetech

CHAPTER 5

Integrating #FormativeTech Into Long-Term Projects

As educators, we know students need opportunities to apply what they've learned in meaningful, authentic ways. When long-term projects are designed with this goal in mind, students can explore a topic with more depth and make connections to the world outside their classroom. Keeping track of student progress during a long-term project can be a logistical challenge that gets in the way of checking for student understanding. With #FormativeTech, you can manage the progress of groups of students, while monitoring whole-class achievements.

In a workshop model, students complete work independently, based on a mini-lesson or direct instruction. Although differentiated tasks may be present, the teacher is looking at similar pieces of student work and searching for clues as they check for student understanding. But what if your students are working in groups? What if their task and/or project looks very different from other students in your class? This chapter will discuss how you can monitor student understanding beyond a daily lesson, during long-term projects, including in project-based learning (PBL).

Edutopia describes project-based learning as "a dynamic classroom approach in which students actively explore real-world problems and challenges and acquire a deeper knowledge" ("Project-based learning," n.d.). If you are not teaching in a true project-based learning environment, the tips in this chapter can be applied to a variety of scenarios where groups of students work over a few days or a period of a few weeks to create a final product that demonstrates their understanding of a concept.

As you move through this chapter, imagine your students hard at work. This is not a silent classroom with students sitting in rows and pencils moving across paper. Children are talking, questioning, exploring, and following your guidance, while making discoveries that will influence their own learning. The role of the teacher is to ensure there are clear connections to learning goals. You are supporting students who struggle to master a new skill, who demonstrate misconceptions, or could benefit from enrichment.

The purpose of this chart is to help you step back and identify the *what-to-look-for* part of formative assessment. In Chapter 1, we discussed the importance of establishing success criteria to guide you when checking for understanding. This process is necessary in both everyday lessons and long-term projects. When teachers are on a mission to check for understanding, identifying the learning goals in long-term projects is essential. Knowing what to look for will help

Table 5.1 Project-Based Learning

	Example #1	Example #2
Real-World Problem	The cafeteria staff notice a lack of recycling in the lunchroom.	The media center needs to be renovated.
Task for Students	Create a public service announcement to show students how to recycle in the cafeteria.	Design a layout for the media center that meets the needs of all stakeholders in the buildings.
What skills might you assess during the process?	• Hook or introduction • Clarity of message • Supporting evidence or research base	• Questions created for interviews • Analysis of survey results • Argument structure

teachers make decisions for interventions, without waiting until the very end of a project to realize *what's missing* from student comprehension.

Common Formative Assessments

Corwin author and consultant Larry Ainsworth describes common formative assessments as "pre- and post-assessments *for* learning that are collaboratively designed by a grade- or course-level team of educators to assess student understanding of the particular learning intentions and success criteria currently in focus within a curricular unit of study" (Ainsworth, 2015). Teachers come together with their grade team leaders and make decisions on the *what* to look for when checking for student understanding. Common formative assessments serve multiple purposes, and you can use these discussions with your grade-level teams to help develop benchmarks for projects that go on for a few weeks at a time.

MONITORING COLLABORATION

We want children to develop skills that are transferable to the real world. For this reason, providing opportunities for students to work together is essential. During long-term projects teachers should monitor collaboration among students. In our context, this is less of a behavior management strategy and more about a fact-finding mission to check for understanding and meet the needs of your students.

There are a variety of technology tools that foster collaboration. Students can work together to create presentations, plan a school event, or storyboard a short film. Collaborative technology tools provide a special opportunity for teachers to monitor the progress of a group and the actions of individuals. Most collaborative technology tools give teachers the ability to track student participation. This is true of Google Docs and Google Slides where teachers can open a document and track changes to see the contributions of each student. If students are not creating or making with digital tools, they might use a discussion thread in a learning management system like Schoology or a shared message board like Padlet to post questions or build on each other's ideas.

Padlet Group Collaboration Board—Students use a collaborative, online space to record their contributions to the group and next steps for contributing in the future.

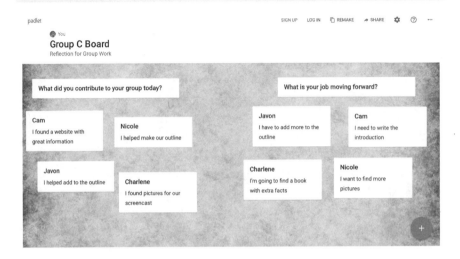

SOURCE: https://padlet.com/

Requiring some measure of digital collaboration can help you monitor the progression of a group project. Although you might check to see that students each contribute in an equitable manner, with your #FormativeTech hat on, you will also look for gaps in understanding. Teachers can review a collaborative document or scroll through a discussion thread to gather information on student needs.

Collaborative documents give students the ability to instantly add comments to their group work—and for you to check in on student collaboration. Teachers in a Google Classroom ecosystem are familiar with the way students can add comments to a Google Doc or Google Slides presentation. Students in a group can comment on one another's work, and you as the teacher can add and review comments as well. If you're not using Google Classroom, you can still have students comment on the work of their peers. This could include a routine where students post their work in progress for a group project into a discussion thread in their learning management system (LMS). Students can then comment on the work of their peers, and teachers can view the discussion thread.

Just like other routines and systems in your classroom, having set expectations for commenting—and discussions on digital citizenship—is essential for success with this type of #FormativeTech. You might introduce an age-appropriate example of *great* comments and an example of *not so great* comments to help students understand the appropriate way to provide feedback on the work of their peers. Although the idea of increasing the amount of freedom your students have might seem daunting, commenting makes powerful connections to real-world skills and gives you a window into student understanding.

REFLECTIONS

In the previous chapter, we examined how reflections could be used like an exit ticket to check for student understanding at the end of a lesson. When your class is working in groups, there will always be a few students who struggle to have their voice heard. A reflection—especially one done by video—is a window into student thinking. Reflection videos let teachers hear the voice of the student who might not be the most vocal and impart a sense of accountability on all group members. If the devices you use don't lend themselves to video recording, students can always submit an exit slip through an interactive response tool to reflect on their learning and the progress of group projects.

Video reflections give students a moment to pause, reflect, and ask questions. You can limit these to a simple 30 seconds if students are submitting reflections daily, or give students

A fantastic teacher story captured by Edutopia shows the power of collaboration between two high school teachers using Google Forms. They created a Google Form to send out to all of their students as a reading response tool. After students submit their responses the two teachers come together to analyze the results and make decisions for upcoming classroom instruction. You can view the clip here: http://resources .corwin.com/ formativetech

Video reflections give students a moment to pause, reflect, and ask questions.

In an article for Edutopia, educators Laura Fleming and Ross Cooper explored the ways social media tools like Snapchat and Instagram can help students reflect on learning experiences. By having students restate their learning goals before reflecting, teachers can make sure their students understand the objective. They're also checking in to determine how they can make changes to their learning process in the future.

more room to talk if they are sending you video reflections just once a week. Students might use the web cam on their device to record a reflection and send the clip to you through an LMS like Google Classroom. Another option is to have students post their reflections as part of a video blog in a space open to fellow classmates and group members. As you introduce video reflections to your students, have a plan for a workflow that makes sense for the learning goals you've outlined and the general expectations you have for students.

Workflow for a Reflection

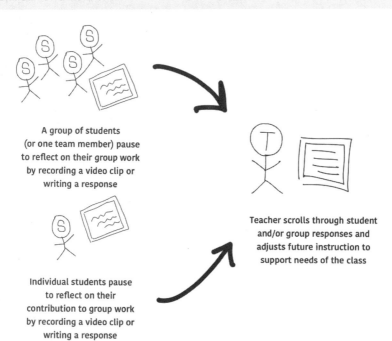

A group of students (or one team member) pause to reflect on their group work by recording a video clip or writing a response

Individual students pause to reflect on their contribution to group work by recording a video clip or writing a response

Teacher scrolls through student and/or group responses and adjusts future instruction to support needs of the class

Video Reflection—Seesaw is a learning tool students can use to document and reflect on their work. Children can take a picture of an activity sheet or creation and record an audio reflection to share with their teacher and/or peers.

SOURCE: Seesaw

Tools for Video Reflections:

- *Camera:* Students can record reflections using the camera on their tablet or smartphone, or the webcam on their laptop or computer. You might ask students to use a prompt like, *One thing I did well today* during their recording.
- *Seesaw:* This learning platform lets students record their voice over a snapshot of their work. Seesaw is a great tool for teachers looking to combine traditional assignments with digital tools.
- *ChatterPix Kids:* Students can use this mobile app to snap a picture of their work and record their voice. It keeps student recordings to 30 seconds or less, which can help children reflect in a concise manner.

When students reflect on their work, they can include snapshots of the activity their group is working on to demonstrate their progress. Students might also create video reflections with the purpose of including the clips as part of a final digital portfolio to document their learning experience. If students are working in groups, you might decide to have one group member take on the role of creating and submitting a reflection to the teacher. Reflections are an opportunity for students to work on the development of soft skills like speaking clearly, demonstrating honesty, and being adaptable.

When students work in groups on a long-term project, it is impossible to sit in on every meeting or have a full picture of each group's progress. The same is true when all students in your class are at different stages of an independent project. #FormativeTech can make the process of monitoring progress and checking for understanding more efficient and effective for both teachers and students. The ability to view student comments and listen to reflections in digital spaces gives teachers a window into what is happening in each group. Keep your learning goals in mind as you continue on your formative assessment fact-finding mission with technology tools.

TIPS FOR TODAY

- *Meaningful*: Examine an upcoming long-term project you plan on introducing to students. How will you know if students are moving in the right direction?
- *Sustainable*: Ask students to write or record a reflection that addresses the question, *What have you accomplished when working with your group today?* Pause and reflect on your own experience of introducing this task to students.
- *Scalable*: Create a list of the *soft skills* you want your students to possess by the end of the year. How can you leverage #FormativeTech strategies to help students reflect, comment, and accept feedback?

Scan this QR code to visit the companion website with extra resources and information on #FormativeTech:

 http://resources.corwin.com/formativetech

CHAPTER 6

Organizing and Analyzing

#FormativeTech Beyond the Spreadsheet

Using #FormativeTech means we're gathering and recording data much faster than in the past. You're now able to check for understanding with more efficiency and frequency—getting a deeper picture of student understanding. So, you have all of this data. Now what? We all know there is simply no point in collecting data if you're not going to use it for a purpose. This is one of the reasons so many teachers push back at state testing. As educators, we want information to inform our decisions in the moment—not data reported months later. With #FormativeTech, teachers can gather data in real time and make decisions on how to use this information within a matter of minutes.

Finding time to analyze data in an already jam-packed teacher schedule is a challenge, but also a necessity. One of the reasons I love #FormativeTech is how it makes the process of reviewing student data efficient and doable for teachers. With #FormativeTech, you can quickly *collect* meaningful data, *analyze* this information, and *make* a decision for future instruction.

With #FormativeTech you can quickly **collect** meaningful data, **analyze** this information, and **make** a decision for future instruction.

In the first half of this book, we discussed how technology tools can be used to collect formative assessment data. This includes periodic check-ins during a daily lesson and monitoring long-term projects. In this chapter, we'll take a look at how #FormativeTech can be used to keep data organized and make it easy to analyze the information you've collected on student understanding. The purpose of formative assessment is to help teachers make decisions to support their students. Technology tools make it easier to examine patterns in student data to help you make decisions on future instruction.

EVALUATING DATA

Formative assessment data comes in many forms. Students might submit a digital exit ticket through an interactive response tool, post a comment on a discussion thread, or answer a few multiple-choice questions on a tablet or smartphone. The type of data you collect will determine how you interact with and evaluate this data.

For example, if you submit your observational notes on a digital checklist using a Google Form, all of the information you submit will arrive in a Google Sheet (see page 42 in Chapter 3). You can look at the Google Sheet and see all of the data you've input over the course of a day, week, or several months all in one place. Alternatively, if you've asked students to leave a comment on a post in a discussion thread in iTunes U, you can look over student responses by logging in to your teacher dashboard on your iPad.

Taking the time to sit back and evaluate data is an essential component of instruction. You need to know who *gets it* or why an individual or group of students struggle to understand a concept. Formative assessment should feel actionable because you are reviewing information in real time and can quickly make decisions that support your students.

Establishing a daily workflow for yourself will help make this process as smooth as possible. The illustrated workflows throughout this book can help you envision what the implementation of #FormativeTech might look like in your classroom. Most often you will use a combination of formative assessment strategies to gather information on student understanding. For example, your routines might include an exit slip at the end of every lesson sent through an interactive response tool like Socrative or Seesaw, but once a week or several times a month you might ask students to create a screencast with Explain Everything or post a comment in the discussion board on your LMS.

IDENTIFYING PATTERNS

#FormativeTech makes it easier for teachers to collect and analyze data. It does not replace a teacher's judgment or lesson plan. Using #FormativeTech gives educators more time and information to help them identify and examine patterns in student data. The knowledge and experience of individual educators is the essential component needed to effectively analyze formative assessment data. The first step of this process is to look at the data you have collected and identify patterns.

The technique you've used to identify patterns in student data will vary depending on the type of information collected. If students have responded to a series of four multiple-choice questions, you can skim over the information and identify patterns. For example, you will take a different action if (a) every student answered Question #3 incorrectly or (b) five students answered all four questions incorrectly. Item analysis of multiple-choice questions is the quickest way to review formative assessment data. It does not give you the in-depth information of a short response or screencast, but it does give you a quick read of the room. Many #FormativeTech polling tools will automatically color code multiple-choice or survey responses, which makes it easy to skim and identify patterns.

Identifying patterns in voice, video, or extended responses will require more than just a quick skim. Teachers should have learning goals in mind when taking a look at screencasts and written work to help you know what to look for when reviewing student work. Depending on your teaching style and personal workflow, you might keep a document open on your computer or a pad of paper next to your device to jot down observations as you listen to and read student responses.

GoFormative Dashboard—This image shows patterns in student responses to a set of questions.

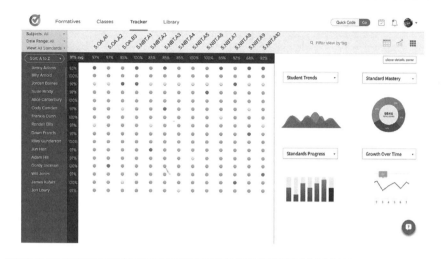

SOURCE: https://goformative.com/

For example, after spending 20 minutes looking at student screencasts at the end of the week, you might jot down a list of common misconceptions shown in the majority of the students' thought process when solving a math word problem. This information will help you figure out what to teach the whole class next week.

Alternatively, after reading through a handful of drafts for persuasive essays, you might jot down the names of two or three students who are all struggling with the same issue. You can share a video tutorial with these two or three students who need extra support or pull them together during the next class period to review a particular skill more closely.

Chrissy Romano-Arrabito is a New Jersey educator and Google Certified Trainer. She uses the "Create a Question" feature in Google Classroom as an exit ticket for students to complete at the end of a lesson. The responses are gathered in real time in the Google Classroom Stream, which makes it easy for Chrissy to see what the students learned and what information she'll need to expand upon in the next day's lesson. This is a quick and easy way to inform her instruction and customize lessons for each class.

Table 6.1 Identifying Patterns

Technique	When would you do this?	What are you looking for?
Skim	. . . when students submit multiple-choice answers or very short responses (i.e., one word, one sentence, one picture/illustration)	• Correct/incorrect multiple-choice response • Misconceptions • Correct/incorrect short responses • Similarities in incorrect short responses
Listen	. . . when students submit a screencast or video reflection	• Correct/incorrect explanations • Misconceptions • Similarities in incorrect responses • Similarities in lingering questions
Read	. . . when students submit a document or extended response (i.e., a draft or finished product)	• Missing information • Misunderstanding • Misconceptions • Level of mastery of a topic • Opportunities for enrichment

EXAMINING PATTERNS

Our purpose for examining patterns in formative assessment data is to make a plan to meet the needs of every student, as they relate to the learning goals or daily objective being addressed. Keeping this purpose in mind will help you work smarter not harder as you examine patterns in the formative assessment data you've collected. When you identify the learning goal, it will help you set a purpose for reviewing formative assessment data. Depending on the formative assessment data you receive, you might tailor your instruction to address whole-group, small-group, or individual misconceptions. This could include introducing new examples or strategies to help students make sense of content.

Kerry Gallagher is a digital learning specialist in Massachusetts. She told her story of moving to a paperless classroom during a fast-paced Ignite session at the 2016 ISTE conference in Denver. She shared how one of her routines is to collect student data through digital exit tickets. This makes it easier for her to look at formative assessment data and group students according to need.

If you examine formative assessment data and realize that 90% to 100% of your seventh-grade students are struggling to identify the characteristics of the respiratory system, you might decide to show the whole class a video clip on the topic or let students explore an interactive diagram. If five students struggle to describe the function of the respiratory system, you might form a small group and have a discussion with these students on the topic. Another option is to send these select students a link to an online module to review the content independently outside of instructional time. If just one student had trouble answering a question, the teacher might decide to have a quick conversation with him or her, while the rest of the class is working on the current day's lesson to address any issues getting in the way of their comprehension. Alternatively, the teacher might simply monitor that individual student's progress more closely over the course of the unit since he or she showed difficulty early on.

Table 6.2 Examining Patterns

Trend	What is the data is telling you?	What actions can you take?
Whole Group	Everyone in the class answered the same question incorrectly, has the same misconception, or has the same question.	• Reteach with different examples • Reteach with new strategies • Dive deeper into a topic
Small Group	Five to ten students in your class answered the same question incorrectly, have the same misconception, or same question.	• Reteach in a strategy group • Introduce a small group to new examples and/or strategies • Send students extra practice material like a video tutorial or online module • Create heterogeneous (mixed ability) groups
Individual	Just one student answered a question incorrectly or has a unique misconception or lingering question	• Hold a one-on-one conference • Provide additional support materials students can review independently like a video tutorial or online module • Pair student strategically with high-performing, compatible student

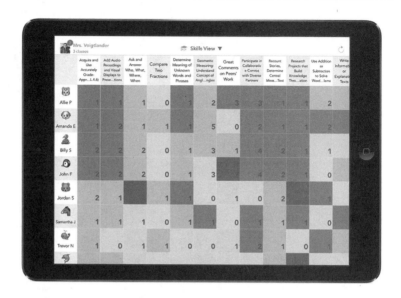

SOURCE: Seesaw

#FORMATIVETECH INTERVENTIONS

Although every student is unique, there are often children who struggle to understand the *same* concept, comprehend text at the *same* level, or have the *same* needs for enrichment. More often than not, when teachers examine patterns in formative assessment data they will notice how a number of students have similar needs. The most efficient way to meet the needs of your class is to notice these patterns and address them strategically. When five to ten students in your class have a similar need, you can form a strategy group to address a common misconception, review materials, or introduce a new way to tackle a problem. #FormativeTech helps teachers get a snapshot of their class and make a decision about grouping. Forming strategy groups is an action teachers can take after examining patterns in formative assessment data gathered with technology tools.

Technology tools such as Newsela give teachers access to materials that are "just right" for students. Formative assessment data can help teachers figure out which type of reading passage is the right level for their students.

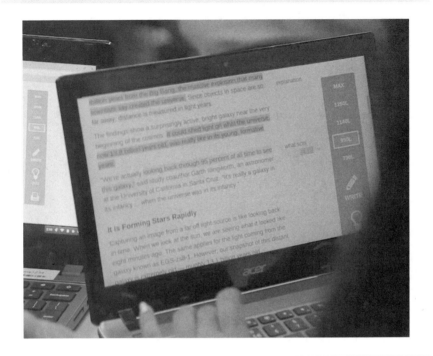

SOURCE: ©2016 Newsela

The color-coded answers of a spreadsheet of multiple choice responses or the short answers submitted with an interactive response tool provides actionable information for teachers.

When do strategy groups take place? Strategy groups could meet for 10–20 minutes, depending on a handful of variables. In an elementary school, a teacher might pull a small group of students, while the rest of the class works independently or with a partner on another task. In middle school, a teacher might call over a handful of students, while the rest of the class works in groups to apply a new skill. In high school, a teacher might schedule a meeting with a strategy group during an afterschool study session or during study hall.

Technology tools can add another layer to a teacher's plan for intervention. When students demonstrate difficulty with

| Studens answer multiple-choice questions | Teacher reviews student responses and sees four students answered the same question incorrectly | Teacher sends students who need extra help a tutorial to watch with a new set of multiple-choice questions | Teacher meets with students who demonstrate they still need extra help after watching a tutorial |

a task, teachers can use digital tools to intervene. Students can watch a tutorial or work through an online module when they demonstrate a need for additional practice. #FormativeTech helps teachers gather data more effectively and efficiently. Technology tools make it easier for teachers to distribute personalized intervention to students in a consistent and strategic manner. In middle school, a teacher might send a helpful video or screencast to a student through an LMS after using #FormativeTech to identify students who could benefit from extra resources. In elementary school, if #FormativeTech data has shown the teacher a group of students need to build background knowledge on a topic, he or she might play a video for a small group of students to show them the setting of a read-aloud book.

When teachers review formative assessment data collected before, during or after a lesson, they might see that just one or two students are struggling to understand a concept. If there are individual students with unique needs, they will require support outside of a whole-group or small-group setting.

LEVELED TASKS WITH #FORMATIVETECH

When you examine patterns in formative assessment data, you may find there are students who are below mastery, approaching

Lisa Neihouse is a high school teacher in Arkansas who uses the information collected through Newsela quizzes to form groups in her class. Newsela is a website and mobile app with current events articles. Teachers can assign questions to students to check for understanding and give them quick access to reading passages. Newsela includes different reading levels of the same article so Lisa can have all of her students read the "same" current events article at their personal reading level.

mastery, and students who have mastered a skill. Most often, this breakdown will not be clear thirds of your class, but a rough mix of students in all three of these categories. Although formative assessment data can help teachers group students for small-group interventions, it can also help teachers divide a class into levels or tiers. Creating leveled or tiered tasks is a strategic way of meeting the needs of students. You can support students who need extra practice and challenge students who have demonstrated mastery.

Imagine you have collected formative assessment data over the course of a unit. As you prepare students to dive deeper into the subject matter, you review the data and identify which students have mastered the concepts (Group A), who is working toward mastery at a grade-appropriate pace (Group B), and who is struggling to understand the concepts (Group C).

Teachers can use this information to create leveled tasks for students. As students work to understand a concept like cell structure in science class, the leveled tasks might look as follows:

- Group A: Watch a BrainPOP video and use an interactive graphic organizer to collect facts about animal and plant cells.
- Group B: Use a screencasting tool like Explain Everything to create a tutorial that explains the difference between animal and plant cells.
- Group C: Watch a Khan Academy video on a related topic like stem cells research. Students can summarize the key points of the video and collect images to create an informational poster with the graphic design tool Canva.

In the #FormativeTech cycle teachers use technology tools for a quick check for student understanding. They then design activities or interventions to meet their needs before reassessing to see which students have now mastered content and who still needs support.

Students in need of individual support can benefit from interventions with technology. As a teacher, your experience and content knowledge will help you understand the appropriate type of support for individual students. This could include audio feedback sent to a student where teachers can quickly respond to a question or offer advice. Teachers can use collaborative or shared documents to check-in on an individual student's progress and leave comments and feedback within their digital work. #FormativeTech makes it easier for teachers to review and support individual students as a result of more efficient means of communication. In addition to an increased frequency and quality of correspondence, teachers can connect students with virtual tools to support their learning outside the classroom walls. Video tutorials, online practice modules, and interactive reading materials can all help students who need personalized instruction.

We started this book imagining formative assessment as a cycle. The collection of data with #FormativeTech ensures every student voice is heard. Technology tools help check for understanding with the quiet students who may not raise their hand, or the learners in your class who participate inconsistently. When you are reteaching a lesson, conducting a strategy group session, or conferring with students one-on-one, you will continue to collect formative assessment data. With #FormativeTech, the process of organizing and analyzing data is more efficient and actionable, so teachers can spend more time designing strategic, personalized interventions for students.

TIPS FOR TODAY

- *Meaningful*: Review student responses to a set of multiple-choice questions. Identify which students need additional support.
- *Sustainable*: Take a traditional task and level it into three tiers. How can you continue this process once every month or once every unit to address varying levels of mastery in your class?
- *Scalable*: Review formative assessment data collected by individual teachers as a grade-level team. How can you work as a group to address the needs of all students on your grade level?

Scan this QR code to visit the companion website with extra resources and information on #FormativeTech:

http://resources.corwin.com/formativetech

CHAPTER 7

Communicating With Families

Using Tech to Inform

Throughout #FormativeTech, we've stressed the importance of collecting data and providing feedback to students. Another important stakeholder in the success of your students is their families. #FormativeTech can make data collection and analysis more efficient and relevant for both teachers and students. Technology tools such as text messages, mobile apps, and emails, as well as face-to-face conversations enhance interactions with families and help keep them *in the loop* about their child's academic experience. This is more than communicating information about field trips or school assemblies. Teachers can use technology tools to share specific information on student progress to celebrate achievements and make a plan for strategic intervention.

When designing a plan for sharing formative assessment data with families, take stock of the type of technology parents have access to at home. In order for parent communication to be effective, teachers need to reach families where they are. In this chapter, we'll examine how teachers can provide a few options to families. There are a variety of ways families can *log in* and stay up to date with their child's progress.

Families and schools are partners in a child's learning journey. As educators, we want to make sure we are helping parents and caregivers support their children in and out of school. Throughout this book, we've established that the purpose of formative assessment is to give teachers information to help make instructional decisions. With #FormativeTech, you can collect information quickly and share it with families using just a few taps of your screen. The data you collect as you check for understanding includes information families can use to support their child at home.

FAMILY ENGAGEMENT

It is essential that families understand the important role they play in their child's education. Teachers can make it easier for families to check in on their child's progress at school and take action. Just like teachers provide feedback to students that is relevant and actionable, sharing student success or struggles should include a reference to next steps. It should answer questions from parents like, *How do I help my child?* and *What do I do with this information?*

Establishing ways to share formative assessment data with families can help parents become learning partners. The most important part of this process is not sending families a copy of test results, but providing resources they can use to help support their child's growth. Teachers can share information with families that translates into action. Forget the test score—what can families do to help their child strengthen his or her understanding and application of content?

Larry Reiff is an English Language Arts teacher on Long Island, New York. He knows that most teachers think of iTunes U as a tool for delivering content to students. Larry likes to use iTunes U to bring parents into his classroom. In the beginning of the school year, Larry asks every parent with an iOS device to enroll in his course. It brings families into the classroom, and they see every assignment and every lesson. Families no longer have to ask their children, "What did you do in school today?" because they already have the answer. Larry's students have told him that, because of this transparency, classwork is often a topic for dinner conversation with their family.

Table 7.1 Engagement Strategies

Family Comfort Level and/or Access to Technology	Teacher Role	Family Role
No access to technology	Teacher uses #FormativeTech to collect formative assessment data and shares relevant and actionable information with families in a telephone call, note home, or face-to-face meetings.	Families check in periodically with their teacher, scheduling meetings to discuss their child's progress.
Access to text messages	Teacher shares information on student progress in a note home or on an online portal. They send a text message reminder to parents to encourage them to review this information.	Families know a special text message from their child's teacher means there is new information coming home (or posted online) about their child's progress in school.
Access to smartphones or web browsers	Teachers can share pictures of student work in a stream so families can view their child's progress and have a window into their day.	Families can set up alerts on their smartphones and receive notifications when new student work is posted.

PARENT–TEACHER CONFERENCES

One of the most common ways for families to check in on their child's progress over the course of the school year is parent–teacher conferences. #FormativeTech empowers teachers with data that is well organized and relevant. If you regularly share information with parents through technology channels, the conversations at parent–teacher conferences will be more meaningful. The time you meet with families can be used to build relationships, share strategies, and design an action plan for each child in your class instead of giving them an update. Consistent sharing of information and transparency of learning goals means you are saving time in parent–teacher meetings for more meaningful conversations.

Easily accessible, relevant data takes the pressure off of potentially high-stress situations like parent–teacher conferences. Even if you are just starting your journey to open and regular communication with families, you can have a spreadsheet with data from a Google Form checklist or an Explain Everything screencast created by a student, at your side as you talk to families. Sharing this evidence of student success and struggles can help you communicate goals for students and help families understand their role in supporting their child's academic growth outside of school.

Table 7.2 Parent-Teacher Conference Strategies

Grade	Teacher Talking Point	#FormativeTech Evidence	Teacher Tech Suggestion to Families
First	Maria is struggling with her letter name recognition.	A replay of a screencast created in Seesaw shows Maria struggling to name letters of the alphabet.	Try using an interactive letter recognition app like Intro to Letters by Montessorium, which prompts Maria to record her voice as each letter appears on the screen.
Sixth	Jamel has mastered grade-level algebra concepts.	Digital exit slips from this unit show Jamel is answering questions fully and in detail.	Introduce Jamel to enrichment activities at home and use Khan Academy or online tutorials to help him work through these challenging modules.
Tenth	Lou is having difficulty working with other members of his research team.	Comments inside a shared document show Lou is having difficultly responding to constructive criticism.	Share the collection of growth mindset videos developed by ClassDojo and available on YouTube. Check in with Lou periodically to better understand his frustration and discuss strategies for accepting feedback.

Seesaw is a learning tool where students can snap a picture of an activity or create a screencast to submit their classwork to their teachers. Teachers can then decide which items to share with family members. Families can use the Seesaw app on their smartphone to set up notifications for each time their child has new work for them to view.

SOURCE: Seesaw

ClassTag is a parent communication tool that teachers can use to stay in touch with families throughout the school year. In addition to sending messages, ClassTag can be used to schedule parent–teacher conferences.

SOURCE: www.ClassTag.com

#FORMATIVETECH

As you communicate learning goals with families, keep in mind that many parents don't know where to go to find help. Formative assessment data collected in a classroom and analyzed by a teacher can be used to recommend interventions and enrichment activities outside of school time. The idea of searching on YouTube for a tutorial might come naturally to you and I me, but this could be a novel idea for the families of your students.

New York City elementary school teacher Rebecca Karow uses the family communication tool ClassTag to share information with families. Having an open channel of communication makes it easier for Rebecca to share updates on student progress and extra resources for families. She can see which families have read her messages on their personal devices and figure out if she needs to reach families with a phone call or meeting at the school.

Communicating expectations and current levels of student progress is necessary to create partnerships between schools and families. Establishing clear channels of communication and consistently update families with relevant and actionable information is a must. #FormativeTech tools make it easier for teachers to share relevant, actionable information with families.

TIPS FOR TODAY

- *Meaningful*: Decide what type of formative assessment data is useful for families. How will you communicate this to the families of your students?
- *Sustainable*: Decide on the frequency of communication that makes sense for the families of your students and your schedule. How can you maintain consistency with updates throughout the school year?
- *Scalable*: Investigate schoolwide technology tools for communicating with families. How can your school commit to keeping families informed in a way that honors the needs of all community stakeholders?

Scan this QR code to visit the companion website with extra resources and information on #FormativeTech:

http://resources.corwin.com/formativetech

Conclusion

Formative assessment is a powerful practice teachers use to ensure they are meeting the needs of their students. As technology innovations are brought into classrooms, educators can transform traditional teaching and learning. With formative assessment tools and strategies, you can take your instruction to the next level.

Picking up this book and diving into the text is the first step on your #FormativeTech journey. To make this work *meaningful, sustainable,* and *scalable,* you'll need to commit to the following:

- Make strategic choices for technology integration that honors your formative assessment goals and aligns with your teaching style.
- Choose tools and routines that work for you and your students to elevate classroom instruction purposefully.
- Find a colleague near or far, participate in weekly Twitter chats, or join a Facebook group to share your #FormativeTech stories so you stay on track during the school year.

The time and energy you dedicate to getting started with #FormativeTech is an investment that will pay off in dividends throughout the school year. Tweak the strategies described in this book to fit your goals and teaching style. Use the teacher stories you've read as inspiration for your own classroom practice. And don't forget to share your own tales with the #FormativeTech hashtag on social media.

Good luck on the next steps of your #FormativeTech journey!

References

Ainsworth, L. (2015). *Common formative assessments 2.0: How teacher teams intentionally align standards, instruction, and assessment.* Thousand Oaks, CA: Corwin.

Black, P., & Wiliam, D. (1998, October). Inside the black box: Raising standards through classroom assessment. *Phi Delta Kappa, 80*(2), 130–149.

Fisher, D., & Frey, N. (2011). Check for understanding. *Principal Leadership, 12*(1), 60–62.

Greenstein, L. (2010). *What teachers really want to know about formative assessment.* Alexandria, VA: ASCD.

Pearson, P. D., & Gallagher, M. C. (1983). The instruction of reading comprehension. *Contemporary Educational Psychology, 8,* 317–344.

Popham, W. J. (2008). *Transformative assessment.* Alexandria, VA: ASCD.

Project-based learning. (n.d). Retrieved from http://www.edutopia.org/project-based-learning

Richards, R., & Meier, E. B. (2016). Leveraging mobile devices for qualitative formative assessment. In D. Mentor (Ed.), *Handbook of research on mobile learning in contemporary classrooms* (pp. 94–115). Hershey, PA: IGI Global.

Index

A SAGE Publishing Company

CORWIN HAS ONE MISSION: to enhance education through intentional professional learning.

We build long-term relationships with our authors, educators, clients, and associations who partner with us to develop and continuously improve the best evidence-based practices that establish and support lifelong learning.